T0146531

The Choir that Couldn't Sing

AND
OTHER MERRY TALES

by

Bob Reed

HOWARD
PUBLISHING CO

Our purpose at Howard Publishing is to:
- *Increase faith in the hearts of growing Christians*
- *Inspire holiness in the lives of believers*
- *Instill hope in the hearts of struggling people everywhere*

Because He's coming again!

The Choir That Couldn't Sing and Other Merry Tales © 2004 by Bob Reed
All rights reserved. Printed in the United States of America
Published by Howard Publishing Co., Inc.
3117 North 7th Street, West Monroe, Louisiana 71291-2227
www.howardpublishing.com

04 05 06 07 08 09 10 11 12 13   10 9 8 7 6 5 4 3 2 1

Edited by Ramona Cramer Tucker
Interior design by John Mark Luke Designs
Cover design and illustration by Dennis Hill
Interior illustrations by Rex Bohn

ISBN: 1-58229-399-6   ISBN: 978-1-58229-399-6

*This collection is dedicated
to the memory of my big brother, Warren,
the inspiration for the story
"The Great Episcopalian Bear Hunt"
and to the memory of Vernon Bronson,
the inspiration for the story "Too Fat for Paopao."*

Contents

Contents

Preface

There is, I'm told, a science called *gelotology*—"the study of laughter." One wag said it was probably invented by a Presbyterian, for only someone so serious about everything could wonder so seriously about what makes us laugh.

Way before Christianity, however, some great minds pondered that question. Aristophanes practiced his humor theories in his comedies, and Aristotle suggested that we find fun in the incongruous and followed that thought in many of his writings.

Later, Freud wrote extensively on the subject, musing that we laugh on an average of sixteen times a day, while smiling at triviality from a superior angle.

But Goethe probably got to the heart of humor best when he observed that men show their character most clearly by what they find amusing.

If that is true, then hopefully this collection of little yarns with a Christian sensibility will be found somewhat amusing by members of many denominations and faiths. Perhaps they will find an ecumenical chuckle here.

But needless to say, the folk or institutions depicted in this effort are fictitious or are used fictitiously. No real resemblance to anyone living is intended.

If some characters seem familiar, however, then perhaps it's a reflection of our ability to find some humor in our own Christian persona. Perhaps there is some buoyant laughter among our too-often pious posturings. It is also hoped that these little stories will be (to borrow a phrase from writer Barry Sender) "a reminder of the conspiracy of life that people enjoy with each other and with God."

This collection is intended to lift the spirit and celebrate life with tales that enrich the soul, while also serving as a little pimple on the nose of mainstream religion. For by enjoying the healthy humor in the living of a Christian life, we honor Him and ourselves. Reinhold Niebuhr said it best: "Humor is the prelude to faith, and laughter the beginning of prayer."

Acknowledgments

Some wonderful folk offered ideas or took a look at the stories in this collection and corrected and improved them. Among them were Ron and Marcia Mercer, Shirlee and Dave Nelson, Eloise Latino, Jeannette Reed, Pamela Otte, Harlow Larsen, Karen Lewis, David Gillmore, Jim Fellows, the Reverends Bill Rambo, Doyne Michie, and Judy Short, and Father Kevin Berry. I am deeply appreciative and hope they will not think I have put their help to unholy use.

And this little tome couldn't have been published without the great editing skills of my wife and of Ramona Cramer Tucker.

None of the above, however, are responsible for any of the thoughts in this little effort, or any errors of commission or omission. They are the author's alone.

The Choir that Couldn't Sing

It all started with one little boy. Then a bunch of folks got together to help him. They were all—to be charitable about it—a bit off-center. And not one could carry a tune.

There was no musical talent in any of their bones. Not a lick. Nada. When they tried to sing, it was a disaster. It wasn't just that they sang off-key. They sang in no recognizable key whatsoever. Each warbled off in his or her own tone-deaf way. So they sounded just awful!

But they were a choir. A different sort of choir. A choir that couldn't—and normally didn't—sing.

Their lack of musical talent didn't really matter very much. But how they came to be and what they did and how they influenced a whole bunch of other people is something of a tale.

In their aggregate, they were an uncommon group of folks who were pretty much out of the mainstream of American life. Some were physically off-putting. Some had their own agendas that did not coincide with the ones favored by their fellow church members. And some were seriously weird!

Not that they were dumb—at least most of them. Or particularly inept—at least most of them. Or truly eccentric—at least most of them.

But they were a bunch of folks who were simply a bit unhinged. One repeatedly stumbled over his own feet. Another lisped and spewed saliva over people when he got excited. One lady had an unpronounceable name. Another one was so slow that she needed a recipe to make ice cubes.

They were, in all, a wondrous bunch, looked upon by their fellow church members as people who resided somewhere beyond the circle of normalcy. But their actions were enough to start small campfires of spiritual hope for a lot of other folks.

It wasn't that the suburban church they belonged to didn't have ANY choir. This was not one of those churches where anyone who could see their breath in a mirror was a member of the choir.

On the contrary, the music program of the Grace United Methodist Church and its Chancel Choir was the envy of all the neighboring churches. The thirty-voice aggregation boasted many public-school music teachers and was led by an assistant professor of music from a nearby college. The teachers were all fine instrumentalists and as a result, flute duets, a harp, and even string quartets were heard occasionally during worship services.

The organist was especially accomplished and could fake anything. He was particularly adept at providing background music during Communion services, a skill he had picked up while playing for the many Saturday morning Masses in a Catholic church while working his way through college. His noodling sounded sacred, but was simply chords strung together in an impromptu sort of sonata.

He always timed the music to the movement of the Communion servers and their pass-the-bread-and-grape-juice-through-the-congregation perambulations. He often had to draw out a final chord resolution for more than two minutes while waiting for one of the slower ushers to return to the pulpit area with his tray of the little glasses.

And the organist was most capable of covering up his mistakes. On the occasions when his fingers failed to hit the right notes and eyebrows were raised, he called it "alternative harmonization."

He and the director even had an outreach program. There was the Cherub Choir made up of the younger school kids and the Wesleyan Choir that had eight teenage girls and three boys in it. They were both led by music teachers in the Chancel Choir. And they sent one of their teachers to the nearby Golden Age Siesta on a weekly basis to lead a makeshift choir there that was constantly being depleted by people passing away.

It was by such ministry that the Grace United music program and its Chancel Choir made a joyful noise unto the Lord! They followed John Wesley's admonition to "burst into jubilant song with music" and Psalm 98:4, which directed the faithful to "rejoice, and sing praise." And the church membership kept

He always TIMED THE MUSIC TO THE MOVEMENT OF THE COMMUNION SERVERS AND THEIR PASS-THE-BREAD-AND-GRAPE-JUICE-THROUGH-THE-CONGREGATION PERAMBULATIONS.

increasing slowly, in part because of the strong music program.

So the proposal to authorize yet another choir was met with considerable concern by members of the Board. Weren't three choirs enough? they asked. Wouldn't they be diluting their success? Besides, which people were going to be in it?

The proposal had been offered by the new Associate Pastor. Although he was fresh out of seminary and eager to make his mark on his first calling, he recognized that the proposed membership of the new choir posed something of a problem.

He had canvassed the congregation and compiled a list of potential members for the new choir. It was, some said, a doozy!

There was one happy lady who was known (by the kids in the church) as Fat Granny Fanny. Her Christian name was Fanny Armbrouster, and she was the widow of Clayton Armbrouster, who had been the janitor of the church for many years. She was also the grandmother of a passel of kids, one of whom was deaf.

The kids whispered that her first name was truly appropriate, for the gray-haired lady had an enormous rear end. It stuck out sideways and backways and every-which-ways, like it had a life of its own—like it wasn't attached to her. But of course it was.

In their adolescent disdain for anyone who wasn't cool, some of the kids in the Methodist Youth Fellowship (MYF) poked fun at her behind her back. One of them snickered that she could probably provide all the shade they needed for their annual picnic in the park. The same smart-alecky kid whispered that she probably needed backup lights.

Fanny had another distinguishing characteristic—enormous feet—feet so huge that they rivaled the fake ones seen on the clowns at the circus. Her humongous pedals and rear end made her amble along in a rolling gait that resembled a sailor navigating the deck of a ship in a storm. Blessedly she never heard any of the cruel remarks, and because she was so kind and gentle, the adults of the church loved her.

The congregation's sole ethnic member had also signed up for the new choir. Her name was Natasha Slesyuahnskia, a Serbian lady whose English was somewhat shaky. She came from a Yugoslavian family whose members were very proud of their brilliantly colored clothes and potato dumplings.

The people in the little enclave that she came from in the nearby city all had difficult-to-pronounce names, and their first language was one that no one had ever heard of. Its alphabet was backwards. Only the church secretary could spell Natasha's last name correctly, and few members could really pronounce it.

What had motivated the lady to join Grace United was unclear. She had merely shown up one Sunday morning and kept coming back; eventually she became a member. It was probably her attempt to become more American—to be assimilated. By joining a church in the suburbs, she could get out from under the cloud of ethnicity that marked her as an immigrant. Maybe she hoped it would cure her differentness and sense of isolation from the American way of life.

Like many folk who seek membership in a church, however, Natasha's reasons were a wonderful tangle of complexity with no tidy explanation. Faith, a need to belong, and certainly hope played a part. And the people of Grace United welcomed her warmly, even though they often didn't understand her.

For she occasionally got her "mix talked up." At the reception for new members, she thanked the minister "from the heart of my bottom."

Natasha's battle with the English language was in contrast to Harry the Hummer's love of it. He was one of the two guys who had signed up for the new choir, and he was—by common agreement—a character.

Harry was on the Library Committee and had the disturbing habit of tapping his pencil on the table whenever he talked at meetings. And when he put away the books that had been returned each week, he accompanied the task with a constant humming. World War II songs mostly. It was a bit unnerving.

Harry was a little bowlegged fellow who liked to joke that he was so old he had some body parts they didn't even make anymore. His hair was white, as his wife's would have been, had she allowed nature to take its course. He was known for his perpetually bad haircuts and she for her perpetually bad hair days.

The dotty old guy had three major passions in life—nature, toy soldiers, and the English language. He loved to spend time in the nearby woods engaging in what he called "power bird-watching." And he was fond of going on walks with the local chapter of the Audubon Society. He tried to combine two of his hobbies by taking along a crossword puzzle and a pencil on nature hikes. But he was forced to abandon the idea when he kept ricocheting off trees because he was so absorbed in his puzzle.

Thank the good Lord he had an understanding spouse. She tolerated—even encouraged—his infatuation with his toy soldiers. He could spend hours with his collection. "At least I know where he's at," she said with a smile, as she sat knitting in the corner.

Most of Harry's time, however, was spent at his typewriter. He had occupied nearly three hours every day for the last five years in a little room in the back of his house writing an epic novel about universal sin. He told those who inquired that he was against sin because he was against anything he was too old to enjoy.

The manuscript, however, was now more than 1,439 pages long, and he had been struggling for nearly 400 pages to find a finish for it. But it just kept going, world without end. He was, he admitted, in a fog of words.

Harry's buddy Murray had also signed up for the new choir. The two got along well because Murray was also short and had an equally childlike hobby. He had a passion for model airplanes—building them, that is. It had been a part of him since his boyhood days. Some people thought maybe it was the glue.

For the fortyish little guy was a secret abuser of stimulants. At least he thought his indulgence was secret. But he had been a member of the church for more than ten years, and a lot of the folks loved him and thought they had him figured out.

Murray was a Vietnam vet whose face had a perpetual look of sadness about it. It was like everything in life was pretty much—too much.

He lisped a bit and was usually shy, but on occasions he became animated, and his remarks were so over the top that some members finally assumed it was the drugs he must be using because of his war experiences.

In truth, his indulgences and his demeanor were a part of—and the result of—his occupation. For Murray made and sold pet caskets. It was his profession.

He had just sort of drifted into it. After his discharge, he spent two years in a bathrobe watching television. Eventually he hung around the streets in the nearby city and did odd jobs and acquired a mongrel dog that became his best friend. When the animal died, Murray put him in a cardboard box and buried him in an empty lot.

But it bugged him. With all the love animals give and get, he thought they deserved to be disposed of in style. So he began to investigate and learned that regular caskets were too big for most pets—unless you were talking about horses or elephants. Those had to be made up special.

So he cleaned up and took himself off to the annual trade show of the National Association of Pet Cemeteries, which was being held in Cincinnati, Ohio. He looked at the various displays and talked to a lot of the people in the booths who were selling pets-who-died accouterments. And when he returned home, he set about learning how to make coffins for dogs and cats and birdies.

He decided to go for the high end of the market. Instead of caskets lined with paper, he opted to line the small boxes with satin and provide silk pillows and even little cashmere blankets. And he was successful—so much so that he expanded into wooden urns for those who wanted cremation instead of burial for their dead companions.

He chose wood because it was, he said, "pretty much God's material." He used it instead of pottery for his urns, because he could paste a picture of the deceased on it or sometimes carve a cross or a Star of David if the mourner wanted it. It did beg the question, though, of how one could tell if one's parrot was Jewish.

There was some satisfaction in the work. He took occasional comfort in the fact that one of his urns with a Rover in it was probably right up there with old Uncle Henry on somebody's mantel.

But overall, his job was depressing, for he had to deal with the wailings and breast-beatings of the bereaved. So he was prone to retreat on many nights to his lonely apartment and indulge in his model-airplane building and the consolation of a "substance" or two.

But his fellow church members loved him and ignored his "problem," even though they didn't know what substance he was abusing. He drew a lot of smiles at the coffee hour after church services as folks kept trying to cheer him up.

Nadine Bodene also signed up for the new choir. She was a "caution," for she was a bit slow. The members of Grace United, however, had welcomed her into the fold even though —some said—she was a few chips shy of a full bag of Fritos.

She once lost her glasses and cried buckets because she said she couldn't look for them until she found them. And she had been in counseling for many years with a variety of psychologists. But it seemed to her they were asking her to forget what she could not remember. Lately she had begun to think that if one day she found herself, she'd be disappointed.

So Nadine went about with that vacant Did-I-Leave-the-Oven-On look on her face. And although some of the church ladies rolled their eyes about her, they warmly accepted her with Christian love.

The last one to put her name on the Associate Pastor's sign-up sheet for the new choir was loquacious Chloë Burke. Her hobby was gardening, and she often provided the flowers on the altar for the Sunday services.

She was particularly taken with a variety she called *pardalianthes*, which, she said, was Latin for "has the power to strangle a leopard." No one on the Flower Committee had ever challenged that.

Chloë talked a lot—mostly to herself. Her constant murmurings were as disconcerting as Harry's humming and often taxed the patience of her fellow committee members. Her mutterings made it harder for those around her to concentrate on the important church business at hand.

Chloë's life had been largely influenced by accidents. She had met her husband, Paul, by mistake. He had meant to call another girl but got the numbers mixed up. And on one occasion after they were married, he had lost her in a big K-Mart and had spent an hour wandering the aisles whispering "Chloë?" She had been in the ladies' room for most of that time.

Chloë had initially been a bit reluctant to join the new choir. "How much time would it take?" she asked. "Would I have to come to every rehearsal and performance?"

For she was wont to go to foreign lands—sometimes to winter wonderlands, particularly in the summer. And she loved to recall her trips in some detail—to herself. But there was something unusual about her travels—they all took place in her mind. Would becoming a member of the new choir hamper her travel-without-leaving-home hobby? she asked.

But her decision to sign up was really made for her. Over the years, Chloë had developed a bit of a hearing problem. And her husband, Paul, didn't speak very clearly.

The result was that lately they had been having some problems communicating. The double handicap had resulted in some odd dialogue:

He: "Did you hear we are going to have more snow tonight?"
She: "No, he won't win."

And one day she told the Associate Pastor that she liked his reference in the sermon to the parable about the multitude that loafs and fishes. Her husband was like that, she said.

And for some time now, she had been singing "where the deer and the cantaloupe play" in the refrain of "Home on the Range." A kindly member had recently pointed out her error at the monthly meeting of one of the church circles.

So her difficulty in hearing made her very sympathetic to the new choir project. She thought perhaps she might eventually go deaf. Learning sign language might help in the future. It was a hedge against the possible.

For signing was to be the mission of the new choir. They were going to be the Silent Choir—communicating mostly through the use of American Sign Language (ASL).

The idea had started when the new Associate Pastor noticed a little lad of about eight in the pews with his mother. He had seen them there for two straight Sundays. The child spent most of the service staring straight ahead or down at the floor with a rather blank look on his face. As the congregation filed out after the service, the Associate Pastor intercepted the two of them at the shaking-of-hands ritual at the church doors and discovered that although the mother had normal hearing, the boy was deaf. Peter was his name, and he was a good-looking little guy who attended the nearby Millpond School for the Deaf. It was a private school for grades one through nine, financed by public funds. Peter and his family were new to the area.

The Associate Pastor insisted that the two of them come to the coffee hour, and there he introduced them to his wife, who immediately engaged the boy in conversation, using sign language. She was a graduate of the University of Iowa and had chosen to take ASL to satisfy her foreign language requirement. The

U of I was one of the few major universities at that time to count two years of study of the system of hand gestures and facial expressions as foreign language credits.

And she had discovered that ASL is a visual language of the heart. It has a fluid grace with small, as well as broad, patterns of lyrical body language and expressive facial movements. Like the "Lovely Hula Hands" song of Hawaiian dancers, the rich movements—in their aggregate—can tell a story.

While there is a great deal of controversy within the deaf community about ASL, "sign" has since become the way in which most of the deaf in America communicate with themselves and with the hearing world.

The young Associate Pastor's Wife had enjoyed her opportunity to brush up on her old college signing skills at the coffee hour with Peter and his mom, and the next week she sat next to them and interpreted the sermon and Scripture reading for the lad, for his mother knew only a few signs. But the Associate Pastor's Wife sensed that something was missing.

It was the congregation's group singing of the hymns and the singing of the anthem by the thirty-voice choir. Her lone voice of interpretation wasn't adequate to the sight and feeling of a community of people singing the praises of the Lord!

So she persuaded her young husband to propose the establishment of a Silent Choir. They would sign some hymns and perhaps the anthem sung by the Chancel Choir if they got good enough. She said she'd join and maybe he could get some more folk to be a part of it. As he went around collecting signatures on his sign-up sheet, the Associate Pastor had become energized with the possibility.

The Board, however, didn't share his enthusiasm:

"Who's going to lead this thing?" they asked.

"Will it cost money?"

"All this for one kid?"

"Why can't your wife just continue on and interpret the anthem and the hymns for him?"

"And anyhow, for heaven's sake, who's going to be in this 'choir'?"

And as they studied the list of names the Associate Pastor had collected, they grew silent. With the exception of his wife, the group that had signed up, while nice enough, were all a bit— well—strange. And the jury was still out on her.

"There are only seven names on here," somebody said. "Maybe we'll get more once this thing gets rolling," replied the Associate Pastor. "Besides, we don't need a whole lot of people."

"As for the money, it won't cost the church a dime," he added. They were working on a teacher at the school that Peter attended (a Miss Penelope Oxford, who was raised a Methodist) to come over and teach the group sign language and lead them in the signing. They would only perform once a month to begin with, he said, but maybe they could do it more often as the choir got more experienced and learned more of the language.

As for the "why can't your wife just continue on and interpret the anthem and the hymns for him?" the Associate Pastor used a quote from the famous choral director Robert Shaw, who had once noted that the choral experience "forces you to conclude that you can do something finer together than you can do yourself."

"And," the Associate Pastor added, "there is glory in numbers!"

His final argument for the establishment of the choir was that it was a great opportunity for outreach. There were about 24 million Americans—11 percent of the population—who were deaf or hearing impaired, he said, and some estimate that less than 10 percent of them go to church. That number was sure to grow. For when the baby boomers reach sixty-five (when one in three people begin to experience hearing loss), there will be a lot more.

"Grace United can begin to reach out now to these people, many of whom are unchurched," he said. "Even if they never learn sign language, they can begin to appreciate the beauty of it and the problems of those with silence or near-silence in their ears."

The last argument hit two of the members of the Board where it hurt. They were in their sixties. And it also persuaded another member who was looking for a new business, now that his vacuum-cleaner shop had gone bankrupt. *Maybe hearing aids*, he thought.

The young Associate Pastor's Wife also submitted a statement that described what the new choir would be doing. She began with a quote from Keats, "Heard melodies are sweet, but unheard melodies are sweeter." "And," she continued, "we shall sign of the great glory of God! We shall sign of the joy of Christ! We shall sign of the summers and the winters of the earth and the promise of salvation!" And quoting from Corinthians, she said that "we will sing with the spirit and with the understanding, also!"

It took an elderly lady on the Board, however, to put the whole matter in a biblical perspective. Reminded by and quoting again from 1 Corinthians 13, she said wisely, "Though I speak with the tongues of men and of angels and have not charity, I am become as sounding brass, or a tinkling cymbal."

And having no desire to be seen as those loud instruments, the Board approved the Associate Pastor's proposal for the establishment of the Silent Choir of the Grace United Methodist Church!

And sure enough, two other folk joined up immediately after the Board's approval.

One, a new church member—Dr. Slim—was a disaster waiting to happen. His awkwardness was, in fact, a bit of a handicap in his profession, for he was a dentist. The tall guy had once been honored for his "significant contributions to organized dentistry," causing some of his patients to wonder whether there was something called "disorganized dentistry."

Dr. Slim was astute enough to be embarrassed by his own physical ineptitude. On one occasion he had turned around and walked smack-dab into his kitchen door. He got a black eye but was ashamed to admit how it happened. He also walked with a hint of a limp. Rumor had it that he'd been shot in the foot by a less-than-satisfied patient out West after the good doctor had fallen down on him as he got out of the chair.

Recently Dr. Slim had begun falling down a lot again and hitting his head, although some of his older patients joked that it didn't seem to alter his thoughts much because his head was probably empty at the time. But his forehead often sported a Band-Aid and his knuckles were sometimes scratched. And even though he moved at about a hundredth of a mile an hour in a desperate attempt to avoid any further calamities, his appearance was often off-putting to new patients.

His caution in things physical ran over into his new church life. He had waited until the Silent Choir was approved by the Board before he joined up because his awkwardness had made his church and social life as a single fellow a bit of a shambles. But his new friends in the church welcomed him warmly in Christian fellowship.

His wariness had been shared by Ginger Ann Sweet, who had also delayed in signing up for the new choir. Ginger Ann was a longtime member of the church who was dedicated to the intoxicating encouragement of amour in all its forms. She had the unnerving habit of constantly falling in love, for she was an extraordinarily affectionate woman. Her mother had never grown tired of telling her that Cinderella had married up, so Ginger Ann kept trying.

One problem was that it was difficult to find a guy who hadn't seen all of her dating outfits. Even though she was past her forties, she maintained her addiction to some Sunday-go-to-meeting skirts and blouses that were (as some of the women in the Ladies' Aid sniffed) "up to here and down to there."

And if her heels were high, her hair was higher. She had maintained her elaborate upswept hairpiece for years after it was fashionable, for she apparently considered hair one of the major religions. She seemed to believe that the higher the hair, the closer to God. The ushers sometimes had to ask her to take it off, however, so the people behind her could see the minister.

Her mother had died right there in the church—well, in the pastor's study anyway. She had been complaining that there weren't enough activities for the young adults in the congregation and had just slumped over in her chair. Right there. Didn't utter another word. Just keeled over.

> *When she* HEARD THAT DR. SLIM HAD DECIDED TO JOIN THE NEW CHOIR, SHE DETERMINED TO DO SO ALSO, FOR HER LATEST CRUSH WAS ON HIM.

So even though her mother wasn't there to goad her on, Ginger Ann spent most of her days looking for wider shores in the lakes of love. So when she heard that Dr. Slim had decided to join the new choir, she determined to do so also, for her latest crush was on him. Besides, she was secretly fascinated by the idea that the American Sign Language might have some gestures for the various words for love.

So it was a delightful, diverse, and somewhat odd group of nine wonderful Christians that greeted Miss Penelope Oxford when she convened the first rehearsal of the Silent Choir. They each had their own unspoken reason for being there.

The Associate Pastor's Wife didn't want to lose her ASL skills, Natasha thought she might somehow learn more English words and phrases by learning ASL, and Granny Fanny had a granddaughter who was deaf. Harry the Hummer loved any form of the English language, and Murray hoped that his participation would cheer him up and keep him away from his "problem." Nadine was looking for a meaning in life, Chloë was losing her hearing, Dr. Slim was seeking companionship, and Ginger Ann was seeking Dr. Slim.

And although all of them had their own little motives for signing up, they did have, in common, an overriding Christian compassion for the little boy they were going to serve. They were united in their desire to do their best for him.

Unfortunately, their best was—at best—terrible. In an attempt to discern their ability to engage in music and at just what level, Miss Oxford had them sing "America." And to determine their understanding of rhythm, she had them try "Holy, Holy, Holy."

Both were disasters, and although she continued to use both numbers as warm-up exercises at rehearsals for a while, she finally abandoned the practice because her ears could no longer tolerate the awful sound.

She began her actual instruction in ASL, however, by telling them that the words in the language were assembled from hand motions and shapes, and the positions that the hands take in front of the upper body. Punctuation and emphasis are achieved by facial expressions and movements of the head. Lifting the eyebrows and sticking out the tongue are sometimes necessary. "So you've got to relax and loosen up," she urged. "Try not to be so Methodist."

And in keeping with their common motivation for joining the new choir, the first two gestures she taught them were for "love" and "I love you." Although Harry said the latter looked to him almost like the old University of Texas "Hook 'em Horns" gesture, he allowed as how it was appropriate.

She then handed out some sheets with the hand movements for the first verse and chorus of "How Great Thou Art." And she taught them the signs for it and began to teach them the hymn.

They shouldn't sing it out loud, she said diplomatically. They could mouth the words if they wanted to, but they didn't even have to do that. They should just sign while the organ played.

So after she took them through it a number of times, she let them go home with the admonition that they individually practice the signs for that hymn before the next rehearsal a week hence. She said they would be performing it at the worship service in two weeks.

It took three weeks, however, before they were ready. They weren't together. Nadine was having a lot of trouble keeping up, and Granny Fanny somehow kept mixing up the signs for *thunder*

and *wonder*. And Ginger Ann's attention span wasn't the greatest. She kept eying Dr. Slim.

So there was a great deal of trepidation when that day came. The senior minister was wary, the Associate Pastor was anxious, and Miss Oxford was nervous. The Board members wore skeptical looks. Many of the Silent Choir members were quietly shaking a bit. All this anxiety seemed to be contagious and eventually found its way to the congregation.

But when the group finally stood up for their inaugural performance and signed the first verse of that wonderful old hymn, they were outstanding! As the congregation sang, they signed. And the second line seemed to say it all!

> *O Lord my God! When I in awesome wonder*
> *Consider all the worlds Thy hands have made.*
> *I see the stars, I hear the rolling thunder!*
> *Thy pow'r throughout the universe displayed.*

And when they got to the chorus, the whole church seemed to be lifted up! The music soared and the congregation's voices rose in glory as the Silent Choir's hands became even more graceful in glorious, grand unison!

> *Then sings my soul, my Savior God to Thee;*
> *How great Thou art, how great Thou art!*
> *Then sings my soul, my Savior God to Thee;*
> *How great Thou art, how great Thou art!*

Many folk were misty and some were actually weeping at the beauty of it all. Little Peter and his mother were hugging and beaming. It was a stirring and exhilarating moment of grace!

The organist sensed that nothing could top it, so he tacked on a quick "amen," skipping the next three verses. At the coffee hour, people couldn't stop talking about it. Folks said it was a life-altering experience!

In the next two weeks, the choir learned another hymn and began to tackle the anthem that the Chancel Choir was going to sing later that month. And they got better, even though, as adult learners of ASL, they had an "accent"—for they formed the signs with less crispness than those who learned to sign early in life. But when the next Sunday came and they performed the anthem AND a verse of a hymn, they and the congregation were exhilarated and again touched emotionally by their efforts!

Peter and his mother started to spread the good news about the Silent Choir. And as word got around in the "deaf world," folks with hearing disabilities started showing up for services, just like the Associate Pastor had envisioned. This led to Miss Oxford standing up by the pulpit and signing the sermon and the Scripture reading and the announcements every Sunday.

She even started a once-a-week evening class in signing for those who didn't want to be in the Silent Choir. And many of that choir also attended, for they had become enamored with the beautiful language with its palette of emotions.

All this prompted the Board to authorize a modest weekly stipend to be paid to Miss Oxford for her contributions to the life of the church, and because she had a CI (Certificate of Interpretation) from the RID (Registry of Interpreters of the Deaf). But even though the Associate Pastor's Wife became the assistant in all the signing endeavors, the Board didn't offer to reward her monetarily. That might set a precedent for future pastors' wives.

As the year progressed, however, she and the Silent Choir got better and better. Pretty soon they were signing one verse of a hymn at every other service and an anthem every month. One night they rented a video of the movie *Children of a Lesser God* and went to Dr. Slim's house and popped some popcorn to eat as they watched it. But they were so mesmerized in trying to follow Marlee Matlin's and William Hurt's beautifully signed performance that they neglected to eat most of the refreshments.

They also began to socialize on other occasions with parties and picnics and other outings. A wonderful camaraderie was developing as the marvelous oddballs "found themselves" in each other and in their endeavor. Their joint purpose was binding the unlikely into a tight-knit Christian community.

The guys in the group began to attend the baseball and football games at the Millpond School, and learned that many historians credit the deaf football players at Gallaudet University, the famous school for the deaf in Washington, D.C., with creating the huddle. They used it to hide their hand signals for plays from other teams who might know sign language.

And the choir fellows also discovered that the signals a baseball catcher flashes to the pitcher and the umpire's gestures for "strike" and "ball" and "safe" and "out" are attributed to a need to communicate with "Dummy" Hoy, the legendary deaf major-league pitcher in the early part of the twentieth century. He had acquired that awful nickname because he could neither speak nor hear. His great intelligence and ability, however, belied the name and put those who labeled him as "dumb" to shame.

But as the number of deaf and hard-of-hearing people attending the church increased, the members of the Silent Choir and the congregation began to realize they had stirred up a hornet's nest. Not all of the deaf were as angelic, grateful, and nice as little Peter. Many, in fact, were quite opinionated.

For the deaf community is divided about their place in society and the way to educate their children. And the Silent Choir and the congregation of Grace United began to hear about the various strategies.

Some of the deaf and hard-of-hearing who came to the services came to protest. They saw no need for ASL. They claimed the deaf should be taught to speak in order to integrate themselves in the hearing world.

Some did view ASL as a steppingstone toward verbalization— a basis from which a student could work toward spoken English and could thus "mainstream."

Others, however, saw ASL as the defining aspect of a deaf culture. They could see no reason why students should learn English or speak it at all.

At the coffee hours, the congregation and choir began to learn there were also other communication strategies for the deaf. There was Total Communication, which was signing and speaking English simultaneously, and the exacting and laborious fingerspelling. Each had its advocates.

All of the deaf, however, had been overjoyed by the crowning of Heather Whitestone as Miss America of 1994. They were delighted that one of "theirs" had made it, and of her ability as an oral deaf person.

They also talked about Evelyn Glennie, the world-renowned percussionist; Ronda Jo Miller, the first deaf female pro-basketball player; and Marsha Wetzel and Guy Kirk, the deaf college basketball referees who "call 'em as they see 'em." And Wendell Gaskin, the track star.

Many spoke of Peter Wisher, the late coach at Gallaudet who developed a new form of dance. To those who watched his dancers, the movements were beautiful, but to those who knew ASL, they were like opera because, in the words of one reviewer, "the dancers moving in synchronization with the music they never hear use the movement of their bodies to sign the lyrics they cannot sing."

At Grace United, a few grown-up folks who were CODAs (Child of Deaf Adults) heard about the services and began to bring their parents to them. So as more of the deaf and hearing impaired and their supporters found a home at the church and some became members, they began to feel less like strangers in their own land. Many began to have some spiritual hope for the first time in their lives.

And the Grace United congregation began to warm to them even more as they began to understand that many of the deaf and hard of hearing were like any other bunch of people. They weren't all saints!

A few were unusual in their own world, as well as in the world of the hearing. Some were even a little bit wacko.

There was one lady who knew all the rules to the old Roller Derby. She wore turquoise cowboy boots, made porcelain cream pitchers in the shape of cows for a hobby, and greeted everyone with a signed and cheery "Yippee Kai Yi Yo" every Sunday morning.

One guy with about 25 percent hearing spoke in a flat Southern accent and was so big that, all by himself, he disproved John Donne's belief that no man is an island. Folks said he was about one biscuit shy of three hundred pounds.

He was a buddy of another hard-of-hearing fellow by the name of Bill, who was currently working on the design for a better mousetrap. He also viewed himself as a political artist, and in the wintertime he stood on street corners selling snowballs that he had autographed.

In a sense, it was a relief for the congregation to discover that deaf and hearing-impaired folks were wonderfully normal in their idiosyncrasies. Because deafness can't be seen, people often don't notice the deaf folk unless they are talking to one another.

In a sense, IT WAS A RELIEF FOR THE CONGREGATION TO DISCOVER THAT DEAF AND HEARING-IMPAIRED FOLKS WERE WONDERFULLY NORMAL IN THEIR IDIOSYNCRASIES.

And the Grace United congregation grew in Christian love and acceptance of them. Even the MYF kids, including the smart-alecky one, had been moved by the whole experience and had developed an appreciation of the newcomers. They began to realize that the art of singing could assume another form.

Some of the congregation and the kids did say that a few of the new deaf folk reminded them of the original members of the Silent Choir. That group identified, of course, with some of the flakiest of the new people and continued to prosper. They were up to (sometimes) two anthems a month now and occasionally a verse of a hymn at Sunday morning service. They had even learned to sign the "Lord's Prayer," and were beginning to be asked to make appearances at other churches in the area. Folks said it was simply because they never sang, they just signed.

One of the most felicitous by-products of the whole affair was that Muttering Chloë was now talking to herself in sign language. Her constant murmuring had been stifled, and that, to some church members, was enough to make a rousing success of the entire venture.

And Harry the Hummer stopped humming. Maybe it was all the signing he was doing.

Granny Fanny and Nadine, however, dropped out of the choir. They simply couldn't keep up the pace of learning so many new pieces. A new lady, Quaint Arlene, took their place and was warmly welcomed by the Silent Choir as one of their own. She wore middy blouses and jodhpurs every day, painted frogs on the backs of little turtles, and couldn't sing a lick.

That didn't matter because by now the members of the group were fond of quoting Thoreau's observation that "the woods would be very silent if no birds sang there except those that sing the best." And they smiled a lot when they said it.

They were also very proud of having reached through the wall of silence and of their discovery that deafness is a difference, not a disability. They were proud of their role in raising the consciousness of many about the problems of the deaf and hearing-impaired. They were also particularly comforted by the thought that, whatever happened to their little group, little Peter could someday look back and say, "Look at what this church started—just for me."

And oh yes, Ginger Ann's romantic strategy worked. She and Dr. Slim were married in a beautiful service on a snowy New Year's Eve. It was signed, and the Silent Choir participated. And at last report, Dr. Slim has stopped bumping into things and falling down.

A Postscript

All of the hard-of-hearing are grateful for the Americans with Disabilities Act of 1990 (ADA), which gives them greater access to society. And for the advances in technology with things such as closed-captioned television, TTY telephones, and the cochlear implant that can enable some of the most profoundly deaf to hear. Some are anticipating the perfection of the electronic glove that turns ASL gestures into spoken words.

And as it turned out, the Silent Choir and its efforts were on the cutting edge. Experts say that in the late 1990s, ASL became the fourth most common language in the United States and the third most popular language class in high schools, beating out such traditional staples as German and Latin. Today some states recognize ASL as a foreign language in high schools that will meet the college entrance requirement of two years of a foreign language.

And there is increasing acceptance of the deaf in American society. The Choir That Couldn't Sing—that signed so well—was just ahead of its time.

The Snowflake *and the* Church Bell

It was so hot you could fry spit, according to the boys down at the He-Ain't-Here Pool Hall. More important, it was dry—so dry that the farmers faced disaster.

There had only been three small rains since the corn had been planted in May. And though the stalks were now near the "Knee High on the Fourth of July" measurement (which normally signaled a good crop in those days), they were a pale and scrawny green that drooped disconsolately in the fields.

The land was parched. Though it was northwest Iowa, where the old joke was that if you didn't like the weather you only had to wait a minute, the farmers were despairing. Unless they got some rain in the next two weeks, the entire crop would be ruined, and with it their livelihood—perhaps permanently!

It shouldn't have been this way. God was in His heaven—or Franklin Delano Roosevelt was in the White House, which basically amounted to the same thing. And he (the president, not God) had begun the New Deal.

The Social Security Act that had been passed last year had stopped the run on the banks, and legislation had started up to create a bunch of federal agencies to help people out in the Depression. And the Agricultural Adjustment Act of 1933, three years back, promised to subsidize farming and stabilize the up-and-down consumer prices for food.

But even FDR couldn't legislate the weather. And while the folks back East read a lot about the Okies and the drought that had turned their fields to dust, the terrible weather had also attacked the Corn Belt—the heart of the heartland and the center of the nation's moral and spiritual gravity.

The drought in northwest Iowa was in its second year. In a good year, there would be some thirty inches of rain and the corn yield would come in at about sixty bushels to the acre. Last year the farmers had some timely rain at the critical event—pollination time—and about ten inches afterward, and they got a small return of around twenty bushels to the acre.

There was very little snow during the winter, however, and no leftover moisture in the ground. So unless they got some rain soon, this year's crop would die completely. There would be no harvest.

Last year five farmers in the area had gone under and "let the farm go back" (to the bank). One guy joked that he had the novel experience of feeding his entire crop of one ear to his horse.

And this year many of the other farmers were so broke they could hardly spend the night, according to the boys down at the pool hall. It was not supposed to be this way!

This was a place that was smack-dab in the middle of the greatest country in the world—a place where those who practiced agriculture knew most everything there was to know about plows, cows, and sows! Of course, some didn't raise anything but hogs or cattle 'cause they didn't like the plantin' and cultivatin'—and being dependent on the weather.

For it was capricious. One year it would be as wet as a widow's hankie—according to the guys down at the pool hall. The next year they'd have to carry buckets of water to the nearby river in order to have a little dip. And then it'd be so rainy they could catch bullheads in their mousetraps. And then it'd be so dry the river only tested out to 40 percent moisture. So the fellas said.

But some years, when nature—and God—cooperated, when "everything was copacetic," the rich, black earth was incredibly fertile! Old-timers said that when the weather balanced out, you could plant wind and harvest a windmill!

But that wasn't often. Most farmers in the area lived on the margin. No one really starved or anything like that, but with the roller-coaster years of toil and reward, a lot of farmers equated continued existence with progress. You never counted the crop, they said, 'til it was in the bin.

They also lived the stingy farmer's creed of self-reliance: any piece of machinery could be fixed if you looked at it long enough.

And in an occupation not known for its urgency, they learned patience. Most identified with a song by Judy Garland in the picture show down at the Lyric Theater in town that said, "If you work for Mother Nature, you get paid by Father Time."

So the farmers lived a life of almost serene routine in a place of Saturday-night baths and Sunday visits. After church they had some well-done roast beef or a "gospel bird" for dinner. And while the men caught a short nap, the womenfolk did the dishes. Then it was off for a Sunday drive to see the relatives so the ladies could have a good visit. Afterward, it was back home for a suppertime of leftovers and listening to the radio. Finally, about nine o'clock the menfolk polished off some dessert left over from dinner—a big piece of pie or a hefty slice of cake.

All in all, it was a hard-working but tranquil life, where on soft summer nights kids could chase themselves and fireflies. And grandmothers could nestle the children in their laps on the front porch while whispering that the bright stars above were holes in the floor of heaven.

It was, ultimately, a farmer's culture—one of public dignity and Christian compassion and as square and straight as the fields they worked, in their love affair with the black earth. That culture also carried over to the nearby town that served them.

The village of about 900 people was located in a pretty valley about 150 feet deep and a mile or so wide. The indentation in the earth had been formed by the glaciers that covered the area millenniums ago. The town existed to provide a railroad shipping point for the farmers' output from up on the surrounding flatlands, and to furnish the tools and supplies for their work. The Little Sioux River crossed under a bridge at the foot of Main Street as it wound its way to the Missouri River.

There was the pool hall, where a guy could slake his thirst; the Kitchen Corner, where he could get a hot roast-beef sandwich, a school where he could send his kids, and a building in which he could find some occasional solace—the Methodist Episcopal Church. The white wooden structure with its cupola and bell stood on a little knoll overlooking the cornfields on the edge of town. Most people thought of it as a place that was long on sermons and short on funds.

And it was the domain of the Reverend Richard Rider.

Reverend Rider was in the fifteenth year of his ministry and his third at the church. But nothing had prepared him for the spiritual and economic problems his congregation was experiencing now. He was finding it difficult to keep up with the things that needed praying for.

There was the rural poverty, of course, in the kids' hand-me-down clothes and the decline in the money in the collection plate. He could predict almost to a penny the size of the collection just by looking over the congregation on any Sunday. There was also the doctoring needed but not attended to and the spiritual malaise and downcast look of the worn-out members.

There were some drinking problems with the men and crying bouts among the women. And the suicide of a member who couldn't take the bank foreclosing on the farm that had been in his family for three generations. It all tied back to the need for rain.

Reverend Rider had prayed for it every day and, most fervently, every Sunday during the morning service. But nothing was happening.

What could he tell his believing members? Why had God abandoned them? He himself was losing faith.

He felt like Gideon, whom he remembered had complained to an angel, "If Yahweh is with us, why then has all this befallen us?" How could this awful drought be happening to such God-fearing, hard-working, wonderful people?

And if they were praying for rain here and the people in California were praying to stop the rain that was ruining their vegetable crops and causing landslides, who was going to be heard? Weren't they asking for some very special treatment?

It struck the Reverend Rider that his special prayer for rain every Sunday was a very personal and individual request. It was a plea that "MY will be done!" and it was ironic to segue into the Lord's Prayer a few moments later and its phrase "THY will be done."

Anyhow, he wondered, *is the Lord American? What if He only speaks—say—German? Maybe that's why we're not getting through.*

It was all too much to handle. Normally he loved the still of the night in the little town when all you could hear was the sound of the kids down the hall breathing softly. Now four

o'clock in the morning was becoming his worst time of day. But he didn't even let his wife know about his crisis in faith, and in order to rest his theological brain, he turned to (and welcomed) the more mundane problems in his ministry.

There was another argument in the Worship Committee about whether to sing "amen" after every hymn, and Mrs. Edmonds, the wife of the owner of the Village Greenhouse and the chairlady of the Holy Tearers Sewing Circle, was sick. The Ladies' Aid had come to him for advice. "What do you send to a sick florist?" they queried.

But his conscience about the drought bothered him. He had to do something! So he took himself off to a Town Council meeting to ask them what they were doing about it. He didn't expect much, and that's what he got.

The Council consisted of four guys who wore the same pants they had worn in high school, only about eight inches lower. There were supposed to be five of them, but in the last election, the voters had chosen a guy who was still on the ballot but who was seriously dead, and the Council had never gotten around to appointing a replacement.

These fellows weren't the brightest bulbs in town. The guys down at the pool hall said the place was being run by the Marx Brothers. Two years earlier, in preparation for the town's fiftieth anniversary, the Council had listened to the rumor that a time capsule was buried in one of the bricks in Town Hall. So they got a pneumatic jackhammer and began probing the walls of the little building. Before long, the structure began to look like Swiss cheese. There were so many holes in it they had to abandon the search, lest the thing collapse.

As to the rain problem, they had also tried to help alleviate it. They hired a fella who had come through town with a Rainstick and a drum, promising that his dance would bring rain. It didn't. They had also written for help to a Mr. Charles M. Hatfield, who was becoming famous as a storm-maker and drought-buster. But the letter came back because of insufficient address and no postage.

The problem there was that the Council was being aided by the Town Clerk, an elderly maiden who had a complex because her toes were too fat. She typed twenty-three words—a day. The guys down at the pool hall said she had about as much sense as God gave lettuce, and that the Council was about as organized as a bucket of worms. But the body politic did listen to the Reverend Rider's question that night. "What have you been doing recently about the drought?" he asked plaintively.

They drew themselves up in a collective and dignified posture, and the chairman spoke out in his little squeaky voice. They had tried the rainmaker, he said, and that didn't work, and they had recently contacted the state meteorological agency. The fellas down there in Des Moines had responded that there would be no rain for at least the next three weeks. So there was nothing else to do. The chairman simply advised the minister to pray for them all and then adjourned the meeting.

When word got out about what the Council had said, it plunged the town and the farmers up on the flatlands into real despair. Now it was official. This was truly a calamity! There was no hope! It was all over!

But just at that time, fate—and Homer P. Carney—stepped in. Homer was the town's auto mechanic, whom the boys down at the pool hall had nicknamed Waitin' for Parts, 'cause that's all he ever seemed to be doing. Everyone agreed that "he don't know much about cars and he's got that all screwed up." For Homer (to put it kindly) was about half a bubble off the plumb.

He had dropped out of school in the eighth grade and hung around town for a while doing odd jobs. On one occasion, he drove the hearse for Mr. Nelson down at the mortuary. But he fouled up a two-car funeral procession, and Nelson never used him again.

The pleasant but somewhat befuddled lad had finally joined the army and spent two years as a dogface. The only time he distinguished himself was when he volunteered to catch the bombs from the army's new airplanes on the target range. He thought he'd be saving the government money.

> *There was* NO MALFEASANCE HERE, SAID THE BARRISTER, BECAUSE EVERYBODY HAS A CONSTITUTIONAL RIGHT TO BE STUPID.

The image of Homer scrambling around a big field with his arms outstretched hollering, "Here comes one!" really broke up the guys down at the pool hall. Homer truly did have only fifty cards in his deck, they said!

After he got out of the service, he enrolled as a correspondence student in the Famous Plumbers School out of Kansas City. And even though he had graduated (and had the mailed certificate to prove it), there wasn't much call for a guy who could fix toilets in the little town, particularly in the Depression. There were other priorities. So he got some more tools and drifted into auto mechanics, setting up in a little garage down by the river.

Homer did live an honest life. The only time he ran afoul the law, his lawyer presented the court with a unique defense. There was no malfeasance here, said the barrister, because everybody has a constitutional right to be stupid. The judge sighed, and agreed with Homer's plea of "not guilty on account of dumbness" and let him off.

But Homer wasn't too dense to notice that what little business he had was falling off because of the Depression and the weather. Though he wasn't a churchgoer, he had heard about the Town Council's advice to the Reverend Rider about praying for rain. And on a trip to Sioux City to pick up some parts, he chanced on a tent revival meeting of something called the Temple of Light, which was set up out on Highway 47.

On an impulse he stopped in. And to his astonishment, he emerged three hours later—SAVED! When he got home later that night, he was flushed with the SPIRIT OF THE LORD! The experience had changed his life, he whooped!

It was all harmless enough at first. But during the next few nights, as Homer went on and on about prayer and salvation and redemption, his wife fled the room. She had taken Domestic Science in high school, and her answer to any crisis was to retreat to her kitchen and cook.

So Homer began to badger the folk downtown. He stopped people on the street and cornered the guys at the He-Ain't-Here Pool Hall and the customers who came to his little garage. They had to have rain right now, he bellowed!

And what they needed to get it was FAITH, he roared! They had to have a REVIVAL MEETING with some POWER PRAYING, 'cause while the skinny little old Methodist prayers offered every Sunday were probably all right in their place, this was a CRISIS! They needed a PRAYER PRO! Someone who could bombard heaven with PRAYERS!

Homer spoke his mind forcefully, and even though he wasn't working with much when he did so, a few folk began to agree. "Nothin' else seems to be working," somebody said. "So why not try it?"

So Homer went around to the Town Council members and

asked them to invite the people from The Temple of Light to come to town and hold a revival meeting. And the Council shrugged their collective shoulders and agreed.

They passed an official resolution inviting the preacher and the people of the Temple of Light to come to town and hold a meeting. They said that there were "sinners hereabouts" and that the "agricultural industry was in dire need of some precipitation." And they got an immediate answer, for it so happened that the troupe had an open date on their way to another engagement. They said they would be delighted to do a one-nighter in the village.

And it was thus that the Reverend Dr. Billy B. Hopewell (D.V.T. and M.T.A. and B.V.D.) and his entourage descended on the little village. The folks there never saw anything quite like it!

One morning three trucks pulled into town with a tent, a lot of rope, some poles, a bunch of wooden folding chairs, and a stage. And there was a field organ, a big white cross, and some drapes. Before the afternoon was over, the whole shebang had been set up in an empty lot next to the American Legion building.

Then the Reverend Hopewell arrived in a purple bus with big white lettering that proclaimed for all to see that "Jesus Saves!" When he stepped down out of it, he was seen to be wearing a suit you could slide off of, and he appeared to have a ton of tonic on his hair—enough to oil one of Homer's cars.

Hopewell was not his real name, of course, but a carefully chosen moniker designed to engender positive thoughts. It combined the two words that a lot of people were out of at this time in Depression America.

The preacher claimed to have been abandoned at an Elks convention as a baby, and that experience had forced him to struggle and strive all of his life. He did have the look of slyness and hard times about him, so much so that when he ate supper at people's homes, the more suspicious housewives instinctively counted the silverware after he left.

They weren't far off in their assessment, because the self-proclaimed reverend was always about one step ahead of the law. In his early years, he had invented some little scams and copied a few small cons. He also became a crackerjack salesman who could sell anybody anything—one time. He liked to say that he had once been on Broadway, but neglected to mention that he had simply spent a summer walking the dogs of some rich ladies on that famous street. And as he grew more experienced in his nefarious activities, he became more sophisticated.

One of his bigger schemes had been to open up a clinic for hypochondriacs. The idea was to provide medical services for those folk who claimed they had ailments they didn't have. Therefore, only people in good health would be treated, and because any illness they had was bogus, the "Doctors of Health" who treated them could also be bogus. They could literally follow the Hippocratic Oath to "first, do no harm." There was, therefore, no need for licenses.

The authorities didn't buy it, but it took them two years of legal arguments to close the place down. In the meantime, Hopewell and his confederates had pulled in a lot of money.

His hangers-on were a ragtag bunch of drifters who were also just outside the law, and they swore by him, for they said he could strut sittin' down. One of them maintained that Hopewell was so good that he could be chased down the street by a lynch mob and make you think he was leadin' a parade!

But the charlatan didn't really hit his stride in skullduggery until he met his wife. She was an adventuress who had sat next to him in the Cadwalder T. Washburn dining car of an Illinois

Central Railroad train, en route to Omaha. After they failed in their attempts to con one another, they teamed up to drink the cup of chicanery together.

She had a sense of order and methodical purpose that had a steadying influence on Hopewell. And she was even more prescient in perceiving that religion could be the biggest scam of all, because people in those hard times were so ready and eager to believe. There was real money to be made in the saving of souls and the soothing of troubles and fears, she said. So she signed them up with a traveling evangelist to study his style and methods.

That preacher had also played upon the fears spawned by the Depression. It was, he said, an atheistic, communistic conspiracy, and good people everywhere were needed to join in his crusade to "Kill a Commy for Christ!"

Hopewell and his wife spent a year in the aisles of the guy's tent, selling some compressed curds of sour milk as "The Cheeses of Nazareth" and peddling a loop of leather with a little Bible attached to it as "The Bible Belt." The corny humor seemed to work, and Hopewell picked up the subtleties of praying for (in addition to preying on) the rubes and the cadences and religious palaver of the culture.

He borrowed his preaching technique from the apostle Paul who, he discovered, had moved around Greece and read their poets and studied their temples and then used his impressions to stimulate his audience before he began to speak of Jesus. Hopewell did likewise.

He smelled around and got some local names and problems and wove them into the first ten minutes of his remarks. When he finally got to the message portion, it was not theologically challenging. He kept it full of fire and brimstone and quite simple, for he didn't understand much of what he was saying himself.

But he adopted a slightly Southern twang and made Jesus into a four-syllable word. "Je-ee-ee-sus!" he would cry. And he threw in a lot of "Praise Gods!"

After some trial and error, he and his wife finally developed a sort of white-gospel, call-and-response service. There were (hopefully) a lot of "Amens!" and "Tell its!" and at least some "Uh huhs" from the audience. And if there weren't, they were not above planting some shills in the tent to testify for those who couldn't or wouldn't testify themselves.

Hopewell also took to heart a wonderful old Baptist saying that the gospel should be "talked and walked." So he jumped and spun around all over the stage with the sweat dripping off of him to prove that he was working hard to smite the Devil. He threw his arms in the air and punched his fist at the sky and bellowed to the heavens! Even the skeptics had to admit that it was a superb performance!

And the money flowed in! Even in the Depression, the collection bucket was full of bills and the gimcracks sold like mad. The Temple of Light was successful, but they usually had to get out of any town fast.

They had spent the last two years touring what H. L. Mencken called the Coca Cola Belt and had seldom ventured this far north. But the heat was on now for any repeat business down south and the marks needed a rest. Iowa was about as far north as any one of the troupe wanted to go. "Any farther," said one of them, "and we'll all be gettin' nosebleeds."

So it was under those circumstances that on the evening of July 20, 1936, The Temple of Light conducted its first—and last—revival meeting in the little town. It was quite an affair!

When people arrived for "the tent show" (as some called it), they were greeted with a big sign scrawled on a blackboard. It proclaimed that the Reverend Hopewell's message that night was titled "In the Tears of His Saints, God Sees a Rainbow."

And as they tried to find a seat, they discovered that the place was so crowded that you had to step outside to change your mind. It looked like half the town was there!

Most of those present, however, were not members of the Methodist Episcopal Church. There was no official or even unofficial boycott, but by common consensus, most of that congregation stayed away. They thought that they and the Reverend Rider were making their contribution in the prayer department every Sunday, thank you very much.

Many said later that they wished they had been more inquisitive. For it was an eventful evening!

As the farmers and townspeople settled down, and the buzzing of voices trailed off in the tent, a lady in a white dress that was made almost transparent by a backlight, began to sing a plaintive a cappella song about Jesus. Then the organ joined in and began to pump out some familiar hymns, and a gospel quartet sang some uplifting songs that grew in tempo and fervor.

The tension and anticipation built. The music swelled to a crescendo, and the lights dimmed. There was a drumroll. A hush came over the crowd. And finally, there in the spotlight, in his purple robe from the House of Preachers in Wahoo, Nebraska, was the Reverend Dr. Billy B. Hopewell!

He started out slowly with some talk about how God tests even good people in small towns like this. He cited Mamie Gerringer's lumbago and Carl Johanson's rheumatism. And he mentioned the difficult time little Jimmy Conners was having with the whooping cough.

He also talked about how the hard times had adversely affected the businessmen in town, citing as an example the tough sledding that even auto mechanics were having. And then he segued into the plight of the farmers.

They needed RAIN, he said! They needed it NOW! And they needed the grace of JE-EE-EE-SUS!

He was building up steam and pacing the stage. And many in the crowd were beginning to nod in agreement!

"Oh, yes!" he cried. "There is a terrible need to stamp out homosexuality and abortion and evolution and the atheistic, communistic conspiracy and euthanasia and infanticide and lesbianism and all the other evils, including the heartbreak of psoriasis! But what they REALLY need," he screamed, "is RAIN!"

The passion IN THE TENT WAS BEGINNING TO FLOW LIKE THE MISSOURI RIVER AT FLOOD LEVEL, SURGING AND CARRYING EVERYTHING BEFORE IT.

And as he doffed his robe and slid across the stage on his knees with his arms outstretched, he pleaded with the Lord to give them some of that LIFE-GIVING ELIXIR! "We are all Saints!" he shouted, "and we are CRYING for HELP!"

People began to feel that the energy in the air could lift the tent! There were some spontaneous AMENs and HALLELUJAHs now, and even a few PRAISE GODs coming from the crowd.

And then the Reverend Dr. Billy B. Hopewell threw in his PROMISE TO THE LORD! They would all become BELIEVERS —even the sinners among them, he hollered—if JE-EE-EE-SUS would deliver the RAIN!

The passion in the tent was beginning to flow like the Missouri River at flood level, surging and carrying everything before it. Some folks were standing on the chairs now, and the aisles were full of people with their arms upraised. The lights were pulsating on and off, and the organ was pounding away, accenting the Reverend Hopewell's every sentence.

He shouted that the Prophet Joel and his extraordinary vision was applicable right here in this town, right now, RIGHT TODAY! And grabbing his Bible and putting his finger on a passage, he read:

> Be glad then, ye children of Zion, and rejoice in the LORD your God: for he hath given you the former rain moderately, and he will cause to come down for you the rain, the former rain, and the latter rain in the first month.

Then he joyously threw the Bible into the crowd! And most everybody in the tent shouted, "HALLELUJAH!"

The few who weren't being carried away by it all looked at one another. What was this "latter rain" business in the Scriptures? Was all that rain going to come down at one time? And what was this "first month" deal? Did this mean they had to wait 'til January? Or just until next month?

But most of the crowd were not paying much attention to the words. They were being carried away by a magic moment in theater when a mysterious power overtakes the actor. Even Hopewell's cynical helpers were astounded! They had never seen him so transcendent! He was beyond himself!

And he was carrying the crowd with him! As he whirled and leaped about the stage, he shouted that they ALL needed to BELIEVE! They needed a COMMITMENT! And in a burst of inspiration, he threw in an old saying he had heard someplace, about the difference between just being involved and being committed. "It is the difference between eggs and bacon," he screamed. "The chicken is just involved, but the pig is COMMITTED!"

And he warned them that if even one person in the village was not COMMITTED, if one soul was not a BELIEVER, if one person didn't believe, if one person didn't PRAY, there would be no rain! But if they ALL prayed TONIGHT AND EVERY NIGHT to the great glory of the heavenly Father, then "it shall come to pass that the sun will hide its face and the heavens will cloud!"

And paraphrasing one of the psalms, he told them that "the clouds WILL pour out water, the skies GIVE forth thunder, and His arrows will FLASH on every side!" And he climaxed his oration with the promise that "the seas will boil and the rivers run and it will RAIN, RAIN, RAIN! And there will be a RAINBOW OVER ALL THE LAND! Praise God!"

And then he collapsed, seemingly exhausted by his efforts, and his handlers rushed to help him off the stage. And while the organ blasted away and the gospel singers sang "I Saw the Light" at a fever pitch, the collection bucket was passed. On the way out, many folks stopped and bought the religious pictures and charms and necklaces.

Most of them were pretty silent as they made their way home, for they had been impressed. And no one was more taken with it all than one little girl.

The Little Girl was nine and the daughter of one of the members of the Methodist church. Her perpetually smiling mother was an assistant to the dentist in town who had the unnerving habit of greeting everyone with a hearty, "How are we doing with our Home Care?" People who were not patients were nonplussed.

The Little Girl was in the fourth grade and had a smile like the morning calm. She was a pretty child with pigtails and ribbed stockings that came to just below her knees.

And she had some artistic talent. In May she had won the annual poster contest sponsored by the American Legion Auxiliary. Hers was a red, white, and blue design with Flanders Field in the background, and it urged everyone to buy a paper poppy to help the men from World War I in the old soldiers' homes.

She liked to play with her girlfriends after school and into the dusk. They ran and squealed under the streetlights, playing Kick the Can and Red Rover. And she was honest. About the only time she strayed was when she occasionally didn't count completely to ten during hide-and-seek.

Sometimes the girls played jacks and paper dolls, and when they slept over, it was a night of giggles, gentle pillow fights, and staying up past bedtime. And whispers about boys.

The Little Girl attended Sunday school regularly and was a conscientious student. She listened respectfully to any adult and was so patriotic that she stood at attention alone in her room when the new national anthem, "The Star-Spangled Banner," was played on the radio. She was pure and naive, and her tender years and innocence made her susceptible to ideas.

The Little Girl had gone to the revival with her best friend, largely because every other kid in town seemed to be going and she didn't want to miss out. They found the other youngsters, and all of them sat together. But while most of the kids seemed to shrug it all off afterward, The Little Girl was still mesmerized by the experience as she walked home that night.

"If only ONE person doesn't BELIEVE," the Reverend Hopewell had said, "it won't RAIN." She knew how important the rain was because her dad had just been laid off down at the feed store. And she determined that she would not be the one person in town who prevented the rain.

So that night in her bedroom, she got down on her knees like she had been taught and prayed for rain. *There,* she thought as she crawled under the covers, *I've done my part.* And she slept soundly.

But the next day, when she went downtown to do an errand for her mom, she got a terrible shock. She had to go by the He-Ain't-Here Pool Hall and in doing so, she inadvertently heard something she shouldn't have heard.

The town loafers and those who were legitimately out of work gathered at the establishment on a regular basis. And they were joined by some of the farmers in their pinstriped overalls with the stub of a pencil stuck in the bib. They came to town when it was too wet or too dry to do anything in the fields.

Some of the guys played pinochle, some played 8-ball, and a few just sat at the bar, staring numbly at the little printed sign that advised: If you're drinking to forget, please pay in advance.

Some sat on the Nothin-to-Do-Bench out front to get away from the tobacco smoke and smell of stale beer that permeated the place.

On the bench, the conversation that day was initially about old Re-Pete Rasmussen. He was the third Peter in a farming family (there was a Grandpa Peter, Father Pete, and him) and, in spite of all this heritage, he was a pretty bad farmer. So he usually had some ruse or another to make a little extra money.

But this year, he couldn't even raise a cent from his staple— the mudhole on County Road 7 that went by his farmhouse. In the past, travelers would get stuck in it and Re-Pete had put up a hand-lettered sign that said: Honk if you need a tow.

He'd then hitch up a team and charge the drivers by the foot to pull them out. The county road crews kept filling in the hole, but out-of-the-area cars still kept getting stuck there. Folks in the know said that Re-Pete diverted water from a nearby creek to keep it sloshily muddy.

But now he had been forced to abandon the practice. With no rain in the last few weeks, no one would believe that a mud-hole was possible. So he had been forced to let the thing dry up.

After a chuckle all around, the talk turned to the revival meeting of the night before. The guys had watched the Reverend Hopewell and his coterie pack up and leave town that morning, and everybody seemed to agree that the revival meeting had been a singular event.

But as one old-timer—Jake Coburn—said, the chance of them getting rain from prayer was about as likely as a snowflake making a church bell ring. There were nods all around and general agreement that it would be a cold day in you-know-where for such a thing to happen.

It was just at that time that The Little Girl passed the group. And she heard the remark about the snowflake.

It stunned her! She slowed her walk and then, bursting into tears, began to run. Blinded by her sobs, she rounded the bank corner and ran smack-dab into Homer P. Carney, nearly knocking him over. The auto mechanic grabbed on to her to steady himself and, seeing her distress, asked what was the matter. And he led her over to the steps of the bank and sat her down to comfort her.

Between her tears she managed to get it out that Mr. Coburn, back on the bench at the pool hall, had said that praying had about as much chance of bringing rain as a snowflake had of ringing a church bell. And all the other men had laughed and agreed.

And last night, the preacher had said that if even ONE person in town didn't believe and pray, there would be no rain. "And those men didn't believe and aren't going to pray. And now what are we all going to do?" she wailed and sniffed.

Homer's face clouded over. About that time, old man Coburn came around the corner on the way to the post office to pick up his mail. And Homer rose to his full five-feet-five-inches and, red faced, screamed at him, "The truth ain't in you, you don't love Jesus, and your feet stink!"

Then he turned back to console The Little Girl. There were some folk who simply couldn't pray for one reason or another, he said. And there would always be those who didn't believe, and it was up to the ones who did to make up for them. And he told her that he had helped bring the Reverend Hopewell to town, and what the good Reverend didn't have time to say last night was that those who DID believe had to pray doubly hard to make up for those who couldn't or wouldn't.

The Little Girl listened and quieted her sobs, gulped some air, and gradually calmed down. And then she resolved to pray doubly—no, triply—hard in order to make up for those who didn't. And Homer said he'd pray doubly—no, triply—hard too.

But The Little Girl politely turned down his offer of a picture of "Jesus in the Garden" that he had bought at the revival the night before. She said thank you, but that she'd make up her own symbol to inspire herself.

So when she got home, she got out some poster board that had been left over from her American Legion Auxiliary project and her pencils and watercolor paints. And she drew a picture of a little white church with a cupola and a bell. Snow was falling, and little wavy squiggles around the bell showed that it was ringing.

She hung it up on her bedroom wall and knelt in prayer before it. The next day she took it to Sunday school, and the teacher hung it on the wall in her classroom. And the teacher led a prayer for rain and then showed the picture to the Reverend Rider.

By this time he and most of the town had heard about the incident in front of the pool hall. The pastor complimented The Little Girl on the drawing, patted her on the head, and said he hoped it would come true. Then he went off to greet Mrs. Edmonds, the flower lady, who was back on her feet and attending church that day.

So The Little Girl took the picture back home and hung it up again on her bedroom wall—and prayed.

Things returned to normal in the little town. It was now early August, and it was still terribly hot. Hope for any rain had disappeared. The farmers, again resigned to their fate, knew there would be no corn crop this year.

But on Thursday, August 6, 1936, cumulonimbus clouds began to replace the big white cumulus ones that normally hung in the indigo sky above the area. And as some lower gray clouds began to gather, pools of cool air began to be noticed. The radio said that the atmosphere was supersaturated with moisture, with a maritime tropical mass of moist air being borne toward Iowa from the southwest. And a cold front out of Canada was approaching from the northeast.

Along about suppertime, a little wind started kicking up; black clouds started racing across the sky. The radio reported the presence of a deep low-pressure system. And about bedtime, great gusts of wind were bearing down on the area carrying . . . was it SNOW? Yes! In August? Yes! In Iowa? Yes!

Soon the wind was howling and roaring, and the snow was falling fast! And through the din could be heard the clanging of the bell in the cupola of the Methodist Episcopal Church!

Some folks started out to see if what they were hearing was true. They pulled on their winter boots and made for the church. Among them were Homer and The Little Girl and her parents.

They were met there by the Reverend Rider, who opened the church doors, and with the snow and wild wind making the bell ring loudly in their ears, he asked them to join hands while he offered up a prayer of thanksgiving. He quoted from Job to the effect that God works wonders and does great and marvelous things beyond all understanding!

And as they stood there in a circle, forming puddles on the floor, he noticed that Homer and The Little Girl were holding hands and smiling shyly and knowingly at one another.

Then the pastor told them all to go home. The storm was increasing in its velocity! It was vast and all encompassing! And even though they were overjoyed and wanted to share the moment, the prudent Iowans agreed that it was best to retreat to their homes where they could ride out the storm in comfort.

For the next FIVE HOURS, THE WIND BLEW FIERCELY AND THE FORCE OF IT AND THE EVER-FALLING SNOW CREATED A NEW WORLD IN NORTHWEST IOWA.

For the next five hours, the wind blew fiercely and the force of it and the ever-falling snow created a new world in northwest Iowa. It wasn't like Coleridge's soft snow. No, this stuff came down—hard! The wind piled up drifts of it in the lee of any obstruction. The fields were covered with the white stuff. And the church bell continued to ring!

The storm finally blew itself out, but not before it had dumped ten whole inches of snow on the area. Most of it was in the valley, which was the ultimate snow catcher. But plenty of the pure stuff was on the ground up on the flatlands, and it began to melt and thoroughly nourish the corn crop as the normal August heat returned!

The freak blizzard (which was now what it was being called) broke the drought weather pattern in the area. More than twelve inches of rain fell during the rest of the growing season, and the corn crop was saved!

Oh, it wasn't a bountiful harvest that October, but the farmers got about thirty bushels to the acre, and disaster was averted. And they were mighty grateful. As the newly popular song had it, "Happy days are here again, let's sing a song of cheer again!"

Some called the Blizzard of August '36 a fluke of nature. Old-timers down at the pool hall said that it had "snowed pitchforks and little old ladies."

Those of a scientific bent agreed with the weather experts, who said that it was caused by a unique collision of moist tropical air from the Gulf of Mexico with frigid air from the Canadian provinces. The layers of air moved rapidly and met to create a severe weather assault. It was as if nature had conspired to empty itself out on a late summer day, right over northwest Iowa.

Others weren't so sure. Some guys said it was due to sunspot activity, the position of the planets, and the effect of the moon. Old Henry Blankenburg remembered that there was a guy from a literary family by the name of Vonnegut who had been experimenting with seeding clouds with silver iodine to make it rain. Maybe he had tried it out right here in northwest Iowa—and maybe it got away from him, he said.

And somebody remembered something from a physics class about—what was it—The Heisenberg Principle? Didn't part of that theory suggest that by observing something, you change it— that the presence of a person could change a scientific experiment or situation?

If so, what if two or three people—like Homer and the Evangelist and The Little Girl—participated in something? Wouldn't that increase the chances of change?

Like Heisenberg, the guys agreed that they were uncertain. Maybe there was more to it than anybody knew.

So when a stranger at the He-Ain't-Here remarked that, at any rate, it surely must have been crazy weather for that time of year, old man Coburn said, "Ah, but it wasn't that time of year." And there were nods all around.

For to a few of the fellas who remembered the roles that Homer and the Evangelist and The Little Girl had played in the whole affair, the snow in early August was a MIRACLE! One that was brought on by prayer.

Lots of people around town agreed. They remembered the evangelist's reading from the Scripture that promised rain in the "first month." Wasn't August the first month after he had preached? And didn't he and Homer and The Little Girl pray especially hard? Weren't their prayers answered?

And they cited the dictionary that said that a miracle was "produced by supernatural intervention and contrary to natural laws." Such a thing was "an event manifesting or considered as a work of God."

But was it really? thought the Reverend Rider. Although he had publicly attributed the snow to the intervention of the Deity, the differing views around town led the Reverend Rider to his office to study the subject of miracles. What—after all— constituted one?

Was old Mrs. Guttlaff's recovery from heart surgery a miracle? And the Hawkeyes' victory over Minnesota in the Big Ten last year? Was that one? Did finding a parking place in downtown Sioux City qualify?

What is a miracle? There were many in the Old Testament, where Moses and Elijah got water from a rock or cured lepers or raised folk from the dead. In the New Testament, Jesus was known for His miracles. Seventeen of them were described in the first eight chapters of Mark. Those events helped bring a skeptical people to the new religion.

But the Bible didn't use the word *miracle*. It referred to *wonders* and *signs*.

Maybe, mused the preacher, *we just don't know enough about what is simply unusual in nature*.

Maybe there really wasn't anything unusual about a snowstorm in early August in Iowa. Maybe, as St. Augustine pointed out, "Miracles do not happen in contradiction of nature, but in contradiction of what we know about nature." After all, nature is full of tender little miracles—like flowers and corn itself.

In the end it was simply too much for the good pastor. The Catholics had studied the phenomena for centuries with mixed results. How was he to determine whether the prayers of three people in a little town in Iowa had helped create a miracle? Maybe Albert Einstein had it right when he observed, "There are two ways to live your life. One is as though nothing is a miracle. The other is that everything is."

So the Reverend Rider finally concluded that something of a wondrous nature had occurred in the little town because of the prayers of three disparate human beings—Homer, the Evangelist, and The Little Girl. Maybe, just maybe, miracles came only when people allowed themselves to create them.

After all, didn't some legends have it that God listens particularly hard to three kinds of folk—fools, phonies, and children? The Reverend Rider smiled at that thought and took another sip of coffee as he gazed contentedly out at the cornstalks and his little town.

Story 3

I Guess the Lord Must Be in New York City

He couldn't believe it! Freddie Phillips was going to New York! To The Big Apple!

He had dreamed of this for years—ever since he thought to be a writer. He had imagined himself in a loft in Greenwich Village scribbling away through the night. And then drinking umpteen cups of coffee during the day at the place that put little frames around the covers of the habitués' new books and hung 'em on the wall.

After he became *really* successful, Freddie imagined himself moving uptown and playing Fred Astaire in an East Side penthouse with a maid and an invitation to every swank soirée in Manhattan! He'd possess a little black book with the phone numbers of a bevy of Broadway babes, rate a good table at that celebrity restaurant, Elaine's, and become a member of that intellectual coterie that some folk called The New York Review of Each Other's Books.

But it hadn't turned out that way. His folks had him measured for an accountant, and his writing career—such as it was—had basically ended with his second year at Arkansas Tech over at Russellville.

He had written three short stories there that "showed promise," said his professor. Perhaps he could go on to the acclaimed creative-writing school at the University of Arkansas after he graduated. But then fate showed its hand.

His hometown honey, Hilda Carol, and he had become anatomically compatible. When she became pregnant, there wasn't much else for a good Baptist lad who'd strayed from the straight-and-narrow to do but marry her. So he did.

They set up housekeeping in an apartment above the grocery store, and he got a job as the clerk at the post office. Over the years they started to raise two more kids and moved into a comfortable old house on Spring Street.

Eventually he became the Postmaster, in charge of the clerk and the two rural mail carriers. When the patrons came downtown to pick up the mail from their boxes, they were warmed by his laconic wit and homespun humor.

Freddie also kept them up to date with the goings-on around town. Like the plight of the only guest in a week at the No-Tell Motel out on the highway. The guy dialed 9 to get an outside line and instead got old Roger Lebbit over on Spruce Street. And when he tried to rent a car while his was being fixed, he was told, "Sorry, Ed's got it."

In spite of the fact that there wasn't much to do in the little village, Freddie seemed to keep busy. He served on the Town Council and headed a committee at his church. And he was usually involved in civic fund-raising activities. The Rotary Club's latest effort had been a successful campaign to replace the roof of the little grandstand at the ballpark, and Freddie was the top solicitor. They all celebrated by "paintin' the town beige," he said.

All in all, it was a slow and unfulfilled life in a peaceful community where nobody locked their doors—a sort of Mayberry with better coffee. Freddie had adopted his country-humor ways to chase away the occasional blahs of rural isolation by poking fun at it. He liked to say that the place was so slow that they didn't get *Monday Night Football* 'til Wednesday morning!

For real excitement, the town loafers went down to the gas station to see a guy get the oil changed on his car or wandered over to the barbershop to watch a buddy get a haircut. And they never planted more garden than their wives could hoe and always held the door open for them while they carried in the groceries.

In that kind of atmosphere, Freddie's literary efforts and cultural interests had sort of dropped by the wayside, although he did develop a bit of a taste for the old Metropolitan Opera on the radio on Saturday afternoons. He particularly loved the Italian operas and their passionate recital of human rights and wrongs.

But two years earlier—in what Hilda Carol called his "menopausal madness"—he had taken up the pen again. He was inspired to do so by a visiting preacher who challenged the congregation one Sunday to think about what God had really said. The Reverend Lucius P. Dodge adhered to a moderate interpretation (in the Baptist way of thinking) of the Bible: Not every word in it was true or the Word of God, he opined. But there were passages that were literally His. Amongst all of the narrative in the Good Book were God's words. The trick was to find them—and then adhere to them.

Struck by this thought, Freddie spent the next year studying the Hebrew Bible or *Tanakh*, which he found had the same material as the Christian Old Testament but presented everything in a slightly different order. He hoped to find more of God's words there and began to separate out the phrases that were actually attributed to the Deity. To his wonder, he discovered that God's utterances really ended in the book of Job (in the Hebrew order of things), although some of His speeches were repeated later on.

Freddie also speculated on what God had meant in His pronouncements, and then searched the New Testament for other utterances from God. All of Freddie's jottings finally ended up in a manuscript he called "And God Said . . ."

He also included some verses about God that came from Jesus and Mary Magdalene and Miriam (the sister of Moses) and a few other biblical personages. But the essential elements in the book consisted of what God Himself had supposedly said, or was quoted as saying. The book was more of a research project than a creative endeavor, but it pleased him.

So he sent portions of the manuscript off to some twenty-six religious publishers and began to collect rejection letters. One or two praised the idea and the writing, but most implied—most kindly—that a Postmaster in a little town in Arkansas was hardly an authority on what God had said and meant. People needed an expert author with some religious and scholarly credentials to persuade them to buy such a book.

But just as he had about given up hope, he got a letter from the Great News Bible and Robe Company in that nearby hotbed of social rest, Hot Springs. They would be delighted to publish his work!

The company had been in business for more than fifteen years. Most of their income came from the mail-order sale of choir robes, chalices, altar cloths, and other accouterments of Christian worship. But they also published Bibles and books that had achieved some reputation and sales—largely in the South.

In recent years, however, the owners had lost a lot of money. So they sold out to new investors who sought to increase and broaden the publishing activities of the company. And the new management was gung-ho about Freddie's book!

They assigned a newly hired editor by the name of Bobby Joe Daly to the task of working out the contractual arrangements. He would also edit the work.

Bobby Joe was a recent graduate of the University at Little Rock, and to Freddie's forty-year-old eyes, he was "too serious by half" and hardly dry behind the ears. It looked like he hadn't even shaved yet. But he was enthusiastic! And as Freddie was to later discover (and say), most book editors are so young, their teeth aren't worn down yet.

Bobby Joe polished up Freddie's syntax and straightened out his grammar, and the book went off to the printer. And he was so taken with this—his third project—that he persuaded the management to authorize an audio version of the book. It would be released about a year after the printed book came out.

Freddie's voice sounded like he gargled every morning with Pennzoil, and he read aloud like a third grader. So to have him on the recording, he said, made about as much sense as an ashtray on a motorcycle. Besides, there were six or seven parts to be read. So Bobby Joe cast around for some actors and a recording studio in Arkansas to do the taping.

But the company had been stung recently in farming out a bunch of work locally. Freddie joked that it appeared that one artist they had hired to illustrate a children's book couldn't hardly draw a conclusion.

The new president of the company agreed. If they were going to do this, he said, they were going to do it right! They'd have the recording done in New York, where there were top-of-the-line studios and thousands of actors!

So Bobby Joe phoned around and contacted some people and listened to some tapes and finally engaged the Bowker Recording Studios in New York City to find some actors and do the recording. And Freddie developed a script, based on the book, for them to use.

Plane and hotel reservations were made, and finally Bobby Joe and Freddie were set to go off for a few days in Manhattan. Bobby Joe would supervise the recording, and Freddie would make any necessary changes in the script.

It was hard for either of them to get to sleep the night before the trip. Freddie kept thinking about how wonderful it was that, after all those years, he was going to his personal Zion. And although he wasn't a terribly pious man, he had God and his book about Him to thank for it.

It reminded him of a folk-rock song he had bought when he was about thirteen years of age. It had been written and recorded by that sweet-and-silly pop saint, Harry Nilsson. His gentle voice was backed up by a guitar-banjo duo and a subtle rhythm section. As Freddie recalled it, the title was "I Guess the Lord Must Be in New York City."

Unable to sleep, he went downstairs and rummaged around until he found the ancient 45-RPM record. Putting it on the old turntable, he listened again to the song's plaintive message:

> *I'll say good-bye to all my sorrow*
> *And by tomorrow, I'll be on my way.*
> *I guess the Lord must be in New York City.*
> *I'm so tired of gettin' nowhere*
> *Seein' my prayers goin' unanswered,*
> *I guess the Lord must be in New York City.*
> *Well, here I am, Lord*
> *Knocking at your back door.*
> *Ain't it wonderful to be*
> *Where I've always wanted to be?*
> *For the first time I'll breathe free—*
> *Here in New York City.*

Freddie was so sedated by the song that after two more listenings, he fell asleep on the couch.

The next morning Hilda Carol had to shake him awake so he could take a quick shower while she finished packing his bag. Then she drove him the forty-five miles to the publishing company offices in Hot Springs.

Bobby Joe had also had some trouble sleeping that night. But he had spent the time reading travel books about the place and furrowing his brow while practicing to look mature and mean in the mirror. After all, he was in charge of this mission and a lot depended on him. He wanted to come off as the toughest man west of any place east.

They were briefed about The City by eager know-it-alls in the company offices who had also read something about the "Sodom on the Hudson." They were reminded that Manhattan was an Indian word that supposedly meant "The Place of Drunkenness." In prohibition days, the metropolis had been called The City on the Still.

The guys were also told never to look up at the tall skyscrapers, lest they be spotted for rubes. They were advised that only a bumpkin calls Sixth Avenue by its official name—The Avenue of the Americas. They were warned to stay away from three-card monte games and never to buy anything from a street vendor or a store in Times Square. They were admonished to carry their wallets in their front pockets and to never—but never—walk in Central Park at any time! And they were told to stay clean away from anybody named Guido.

One lady shuddered at the thought of two Protestant guys trying to make their way in a city where the inhabitants' ancestors traditionally came from "The Three I's"—Italy, Ireland, and Israel. She told them to be careful.

Then off they went—two innocents abroad. On the cab ride to the airport, Bobby Joe admitted, "I'm not so sure I know all I don't know." Freddie agreed. After all, neither of them had ever been past Ohio.

They had to take Ozark Airlines to Chicago to catch the jet to New York. Freddie joked that their plane would probably be one of those where you could roll down the window. And its only safety feature would be a flotation device, which he said was bound to be real useful over Iowa. Both laughed nervously.

But they made it to the Windy City and the transfer and the flight to La Guardia was as easy as slidin' off a greased hog backwards, according to Freddie. And as the New York skyline came into view, his face lit up like a new ride at an amusement park.

Their first encounter with the reality of New York City, however, came at the baggage carousel. There, people pushed, shoved, and hollered their way to their luggage. They all seemed to be in a tremendous hurry and were terribly aggressive and inconsiderate!

On the cab ride into The Big Apple, the guys were dumbstruck by the potholes and cracks in the road and the debris surrounding it. Even though the new mayor had cleaned things up a bit, old tires and stoves and mattresses and stripped and burned-out cars littered the roadside. Zillions of bits of paper and cloth stuck to the fences. Graffiti marred every empty space.

And when they emerged from the cab into midtown Manhattan, the noise of the place nearly overwhelmed them. Honking horns appeared to be the official greeting, and the cacophony of cars and cabs screeching and blaring and weaving their way past the hundreds of double-parked trucks made their heads hurt. The din was unbelievable! Freddie remembered that Edna St. Vincent Millay had once written, "You can see the noise!"

The desk clerk at the hotel was a bit imperious for Freddie's taste, but this WAS New York. Wow! And the double room—though small—was clean. So after dumping their bags in the closet, they set off for the recording studio.

The number of pedestrians out on that sunny day was incredible! Freddie joked that there were more people there in a quarter of a block than at all the sales during the year at a Wal-Mart back home.

And the variety of faces was astonishing! It looked like every extra from a classic Fellini movie and all the leftover guests from a photo shoot at an old Andy Warhol party had come together for some bizarre convention.

In fact, there were more people on the sidewalks than either of the guys had ever seen in one place! Many shoved their way in and out of the stream of humanity in a sort of curious half jog. Others swaggered along somewhat leisurely, looking quite important. And a few slunk along in a shuffle, hiding their faces from the world.

Beggars with their hands outstretched competed with guys in orange carpenter's aprons who were handing out fliers. Homeless people pushing supermarket carts containing all of their belongings competed for space with boys pushing racks of clothing through the streets. Young ladies in business suits raced along in their white tennis shoes, intent on getting somewhere fast with the contents of their briefcases. The aroma of roasting chestnuts and enormous pretzels from vendors' carts wafted through the air, and the babble of a half-dozen languages competed with the honking horns and screaming sirens.

The tempo was so fast and furious that the two Arkansas travelers were nearly engulfed and turned around by the huddled masses yearning for a good day. They were caught up in the frantic beat of an accelerated pace, as the engine that was New York City pulled them along!

Neither could remember whether the lighted sign on top of a cab meant that it was available or had passengers, but they finally figured it out. After politely standing on the sidewalk waving their hands for twenty minutes, they ventured toward the middle of the street and eventually flagged one down.

Once inside the cab, a sign proclaimed, Driver Doen't Speake Enklish. Freddie said it made the ride to the studio a real adventure.

They arrived a little disheveled and somehow out of breath at the Bowker Recording Studios, which were located on the sixteenth floor of a nondescript building on the upper west side. Freddie told people later that the elevator operator there gave them the impression that their floor was out of his way.

But they were greeted at Bowker by the manager, Annie McDaniel, an Irish lady who turned out to be an oasis in the fast action of city life. Annie topped the scales at well over 280 pounds, but she was as affable as she was big.

Her calm demeanor and motherly voice almost made them forget the terrors of the last hour. She poured them a cup of coffee and took them on a tour of "the studios." They were less than impressed. Although the place contained what appeared to be state-of-the-art audio equipment, it was all crammed into two rooms—a little office and a recording studio that was about as big as a bedroom.

From this had come the great sample recordings Bobby Joe

had heard back in Arkansas? The place was smaller and more cramped than KICK-FM, his college rock-and-roll station in Little Rock!

They were equally nonplussed when Annie introduced them to "our engineer." He was a thin young man with a scraggly beard, an earring, and plaid shoes. And he appeared to have made himself bald on purpose.

But Annie's soothing voice and confident manner relieved any anxiety they felt, and the place was soundproof and quiet. After some discussion about the schedule and script changes, they were ready to meet the actors she had selected,

Both Bill and Jerry WERE CAPABLE OF DOING THE VOICE OF GOD, SAID ANNIE. THE QUESTION WAS, "IS GOD A BASS OR A BARITONE?"

who were arriving as they finished their little tour.

The thespians were the usual artsy bunch who had trod many a board. Bill was a big black man with a buttery baritone voice like James Earl Jones. He had just come in off the road from a company of *Show Boat*, where he had sung "Old Man River" in ninety-seven performances.

Jerry, a little white guy, looked like he could use a good meal. But he had a bass voice like one of the Statler Brothers, and although he was up for a part in an off-Broadway show, he told them he was glad he could "squeeze them into his schedule."

Both Bill and Jerry were capable of doing the voice of God, said Annie. The question was, "Is God a bass or a baritone?"

She also introduced them to Craig, a sort of swingman low tenor, who could do hundreds of voices (he said) but who (he confessed) needed strong motivation for any role if he was to do

it right. He could do Jesus or God or "any of those other characters," for he was (he informed them) The Voice Magician.

Then there was Julie. She was an aging, voice-over specialist
with hair the color of burnt sienna. Her eyes were out of sync,
but her voice was pure and sweet, and she said she could do both
Mary and Miriam.

So it came down to the casting of God. What did the boys
from Arkansas want? asked Annie. A voice that was sepulchral
and mellifluous? With a hint of black argot? A voice that was
synthetically authoritative? Warm and friendly? Ordinary but
textured? How did they want God to sound?

Freddie and Bobby Joe stared at one another. They had
never discussed this. It hadn't come up. God sounded like—
well—like God.

But if they didn't have an opinion, the others did. So a heated
discussion ensued.

Bill said the Lord sounded like Paul Robeson, the great Negro
singer of the '30s whose career he was trying to emulate.

"No," said Jerry, "too black." Besides, God's voice was like
Charleton Heston's, who had played Him in a movie.

"No," said Craig, "Heston played Moses!" And he weighed in
with the opinion that God's voice sounded like old Walter
Cronkite. "After all," he said, "Cronkite had been once voted
the most trustworthy man in America, and I do a great
Cronkite!"

The egos were out in force, and the discussion was spirited.
About the only thing the actors agreed on was that God's voice
was not that of a woman. They hooted down Julie's suggestion
that she do the role. "Could anyone imagine a girl's voice making
the pronouncement 'Let There Be Light!'" Jerry laughed.

Bobby Joe and Freddie were befuddled. This was bigger and more complicated than they thought. A lot of people were going to get their idea of God by the voice on this recording. And they had to make the decision. It was a grave responsibility.

Sure, there had been some voice-over sequences in old Cecil B. DeMille movies that made God sound like a basso profundo at the Metropolitan Opera. But this was today. Should He sound like that now—in modern times?

So they chickened out. Bobby Joe told Annie that they would delay the recording until they did more thinking about it in order to come up with the right decision about the voice of God.

Back out on the sidewalk they were assaulted by the steam rising from manhole covers and the yammering of jackhammers tearing up the streets. And they were again whirled about and buffeted by the denizens of Gotham and the rapid crush and clash of cultures among the teeming throng.

Bobby Joe remembered from his readings that Washington Irving had dubbed the place Gotham because it reminded him of the little English town by that name whose inhabitants had pretended to be nuts in order to prevent a king from constructing a castle nearby. Freddie said, "Yeah—sounds about right."

It was the rush hour, and all the cabs had lighted signs that said: Off Duty. When they finally did get one, they had to listen to the new seat-belt safety message from the Rockettes and were frustrated by the creeping crosstown traffic and the ever-upward meter.

Back in their hotel room, they came to realize that Annie McDaniel's little place had been a temporary refuge from their experience in urban survival. After a lie-down, Bobby Joe suggested they go to a Broadway show or the Italian opera at the Met. But Freddie joked that he would have to take a second mortgage out on his house in order to pay for a ticket. So they waited until the traffic had cleared and the citizens had retreated to their lairs before they ventured out for dinner.

They avoided the well-known restaurants, convinced that their yokel looks would only get them a table by the kitchen. And after perusing the posted menus on the front of three or four establishments, they settled on a Japanese place that looked pretty good. As Freddie said, at least they were American and in their own country. And even though he was a dunce when it came to languages, Freddie figured that maybe he wouldn't feel so out of place, there in the Kurofume Nippon Restaurant.

Bobby Joe had worked as a busboy in a Japanese restaurant one summer during college, so he briefed Freddie before they went in. "I'll do the ordering," he said. "All you have to do is remember to say *arrigato* a lot. It means 'Thank you.' The Japanese are extremely polite."

As they waited for a table, Bobby Joe excused himself and went to the bathroom. When he returned he was confronted by the sight of Freddie bowing repeatedly to the headwaiter, who had shown him to their table. The Japanese guy was bowing back, but wore a puzzled look. When Bobby got close enough, he could hear Freddie bowing and saying over and over again, "Rigoletto, Rigoletto."

They had some shrimp tempura and beef *negimake*. And on the way back to the hotel, Bobby Joe had an inspiration! They'd do their own research about God's voice!

So they stopped at a brightly lit diner and began to poll the customers seated at the counter. "What—or who—did the voice of God sound like?" they asked.

When they got back to their hotel room they totaled up the results they had jotted down on a napkin. There were three patrons who said David Letterman, two votes for the guy who had played

Coach on the old sitcom *Cheers*, and one for Henry Kissinger with a bad head cold. Somebody suggested that God always sounded to him like the actor who played the spaced-out Jim on the old sitcom *Taxi*. A black guy said he thought the Lord probably sounded like Flip Wilson doing his classic routine as the Reverend Leroy of The Church of What's Happening Now. And there was one wise guy who nominated Rodney Dangerfield, before threatening to punch Bobby Joe's lights out if he didn't go away.

So they went to bed thoroughly confused—and woke up the same way. The prices for breakfast in the hotel coffee shop were outrageous, so they walked a block to a Greek diner, and Freddie picked up a tabloid newspaper on the way.

On the inside pages of the newspaper, he was treated to stories of yesterday's hassles in The Big Apple, describing raids on drug houses and the arrests of pickpockets, beside breathless pictures of actresses plugging themselves and shots of a plump Elizabeth Taylor. There were shocking items about financial corruption on Wall Street and in the mayor's office, along with a stunning story on an education official who boasted that there were only 4,760 crimes against teachers in the classrooms last year. And there were interviews with space aliens and reports about witness tampering in the courts and loan sharking and extortion and news bits about small fires in the subways.

The motto of the paper said it all. It was, as it proclaimed on its front page, "New York's Hometown Newspaper." It seemed to be a paper that profited from the sensational, the bizarre, and the tragic.

By the time they were into their second cup of coffee (that Freddie said was so strong you could drive a nail with it), Bobby Joe had begun listening to the snippets of loud conversations around them. *Everybody was talkin' lahk Noo Yawkers*, he thought.

It was "Gimmie anuddah cupa caffee anna cheese danish," and "Am I right or am I wrong?"—all accompanied by a big display of male neck muscles.

Bobby was particularly taken with an exchange at the counter between one of the owners and a guy that had a face that resembled a blocked punt.

"Eh—member liddel Joanie? I sar her drawn pikshahs inda pawk yestaday."

"Wot can I tellya? It's fall."

"Yeh, no problem."

"Who knew?"

"Fuhgedaboudit."

"No problem."

And then the owner glanced over at Bobby Joe and hollered, "Whaddahya lookinat?"

As they hastily left the diner, Freddie whispered that the guy sitting at the counter was maybe a son of Muffaleto Manny, a reputed capo in the Gambize family that he had recently read about in the paper. And if Bobby Joe valued his life, he shouldn't eavesdrop or even look directly at people anymore in New York City!

By this time the two had determined that they needed some help and perspective in making their decision about the casting of God, so they decided to phone the home office in Arkansas. Back at the hotel, Bobby Joe got the president of the Great News Company on the line and explained their dilemma.

The president said he had no idea what or who God sounded like, but he'd check around. He'd ask the staff and get back to them.

So with some time to kill, Freddie persuaded Bobby Joe to accompany him to the Museum of Modern Art. There they saw some drawings by Hieronymous Blosch and some illustrations of Dante's Inferno that appeared to resemble the city they were in.

And as they left the MOMA, they almost ran into a little guy leading a kangaroo into the door of the place! The remarkable thing about it was that no heads turned. Passersby simply ignored the scene with New York nonchalant insouciance.

When they got back to the hotel, the boys had a message to call Hot Springs. When they did, the president said he had taken a poll of the staff about whose voice God sounded like and proceeded to read them the results. Bobby Joe repeated the names to Freddie, who wrote them down on some hotel stationery.

Name	Votes
David Letterman	5
Steve Allen	3
Edmund Gwenn	2
Jimmy Carter	1
Desi Arnaz	1
Bert Parks	1
Dick Cavett	1
Johnny Carson	1
Mel Torme	1
Tom Brokaw	1
George Burns	1

"So," the president said, "that's what most of the staff here thinks." Some didn't take part, and he himself didn't want to put up a candidate, but he was sure they would make the right decision, so he wished them good luck and hung up because he had a dental appointment.

Bobby Joe and Freddie examined the list. The names of the

Midwest host-announcer types stood out. They were all born in the Corn Belt and had the wonderfully unaccented all-American baritone voice that was valued so much by radio-station program directors. There were Carson and Cavett (Nebraska), Letterman (Indiana), Allen (Iowa), and Brokaw (South Dakota). But nobody could really tell where they were from. And Letterman had been picked by three of the patrons at the big diner the previous night.

Bobby Joe thought he could account for the rest of the votes. The ones for Edmund Gwenn were probably from the two ditsy girls in Accounting who had gotten that actor's role as Santa Claus in the movie *Miracle on 34th Street* mixed up with God somehow. The Jimmy Carter vote undoubtedly came from George the janitor, who was a died-in-the-wool Baptist from Georgia. And the vote for the dead ex-husband of Lucille Ball came from one of the Latinas in the warehouse.

The nod to the old singer Mel Torme (who was once known as The Velvet Fog) surely came from Gladys, the ancient receptionist. Bobby Joe couldn't account for the vote for old Bert Parks, but he was sure that the one for the late George Burns was from Harvey the Salesman who had a weird sense of humor.

But that last notion got them to thinking. George Burns had actually been seen as God in two movies in the '70s. What other films or plays or TV shows showed an actor playing God, and what did He look and sound like?

Bobby Joe remembered seeing a stage production of *Green Pastures* in college with an all-black cast that featured a big fat guy playing De Lawd. Bill Cosby once did a routine early in his career in which he played both Noah and God. And Freddie recalled an avant-garde television play on PBS titled *Steam Bath*, in which God was a Puerto Rican towel attendant.

Certainly a representation of Jesus had been seen on the screen.

But any visual depiction of God in the past that either of them could remember was usually played for laughs. The voice that was used was also funny. And they weren't in the funny business.

Still, Freddie remembered a 1981 movie called Time Bandits, in which Ralph Richardson played a tough but fair God, and Bobby Joe said he had seen the 1998 animated feature *The Prince of Egypt*, in which Val Kilmer's voice spoke for God. Even in this more secular time when visual images of God and His voice had become more prevalent, none of these images and voices seemed to fit their project.

So they were back to square one. It was way past lunchtime, and Freddie thought that maybe some food might inspire them. But they were so intimidated by now by the prices charged in Manhattan restaurants that they decided to have lunch back at their Greek diner. It had become familiar and safe, and Freddie said that the big two-foot-high menu had more listings than all the names in his telephone book back in Arkansas!

As they ate their meal, they pondered their problem. Bobby Joe whispered that his chicken-salad sandwich had dark meat in it, and Freddie said his meat loaf was lukewarm. But their minds were elsewhere, and they downed their food in silence.

On the way back to the hotel, though, Bobby Joe came up with a solution. They would get Craig, The Voice Magician, to imitate the trombone voice of Dave Letterman or Johnny Carson or Steve Allen or Dick Cavett or Tom Brokaw. He could use the voice he did best. Those guys were familiar enough, and audiences had become used to their white-bread-American-apple-pie voices. And if nobody knew where that type of voice really came from, why couldn't it be from heaven?

Freddie bought it—sort of. It was better than any idea he had. Although he was uncomfortable with the determination, he said

he'd go along with it. So Bobby Joe phoned Annie at the recording studio and told her to call in the actors for the next morning.
They'd use Bill and Jerry for some of the other parts, and Julie
could handle the women's roles. But make sure Craig was there,
he said. He was going to play God.

So the boys had a lie-down, and then decided to watch the six
o'clock news before they thought about dinner. But the televised
news with its fast-paced stories was disturbing. It was "If it bleeds,
it leads" journalism. There were reports showing police cars racing
to a crime scene, and pictures of groups of folks being beaten back
while they protested something. There were shots of fire engines
clanging and pickpockets being arrested. Someone had left a baby
in a subway. Someone else had robbed a church. Everything was
reported in a rapid, singsong way. And there were the endless com-
mercials. Through it all, the cheery anchors with their toothy
smiles and perfect hairdos chatted away mindlessly.

The boys weren't much in the mood for a big meal after all
that, so they headed back to the familiar diner. Freddie still had
reservations about the whole deal and was unsettled. In fact, he
was so preoccupied on the walk that he didn't even seem to
notice when they passed under some scaffolding and a brick fell
to the street, nearly hitting a beautiful young woman wearing a
purple hat and brown lipstick. He was so distracted that he even
failed to notice that he had stepped in a big wad of chewing gum
that was now sticking to his left sole.

The fast pace of the gritty city and the recording hassle was
getting to him. He was in the midst of an out-of-this-world experience and having a hard time breathing. His nerves were fraz-
zled, and he felt like locking himself in the hotel room and
refusing to come out until somebody did something about slow-
ing everything down! When they got to the diner, the boys

joined the line of customers that had queued up to get in. As they waited, a girl of about ten ran by, bumping into a disabled guy with two metal arm-canes, nearly knocking him over. When Freddie gently remonstrated with her that she wasn't showing much consideration for others, she stared at him blankly. There was no embarrassment or remorse in her eyes.

Something in Freddie snapped. Even children were in a hurry in this town! He had to get out of here!

And this whole business about selecting a voice for God was all wrong! *Some things don't transfer well,* Freddie realized. His book allowed the readers to put their own image of God and His voice into play. *Look at all the different suggestions they had for the voice of God! He speaks to everyone individually and sounds different to different people!*

Each of us should make up our own voice for God, thought Freddie. *He's what we want Him to sound like when we want Him to sound like God. People should read the book and supply their own voice for Him and not listen to someone else's version!*

Freddie pulled Bobby Joe aside and explained it all to him. He couldn't go through with the recording. And he had to get out of this city—*now!*

He wasn't completely surprised when Bobby Joe agreed. The young editor had been even more serious and quiet since they had decided that Craig should play God, as if his decision about the voice of God was weighing him down. And he said they should probably get out of this place where even purple-hatted female angels could get damaged by falling bricks, and go back to where the birds were chirping and visitors to town took off their shoes so they wouldn't wake everybody else up.

So they skipped dinner and made a quick call to make sure

that Annie was still at the recording studio. She was working late, and she agreed to wait for them, so they cabbed over to explain things to her right that evening. This time the elevator operator greeted them with the directive "ALLTHEWAY-BACKANDFACETHEFRONT."

When they got upstairs, they told Annie that they wouldn't be doing the recording after all, but that they'd pay her and the actors for their time and expenses to date. She took it quite well.

"Some things aren't suited for some things," Annie said. And she told them of an incident that happened back in Wisconsin when she was a young educational television director at the university station in Madison.

For many years, the statewide network of noncommercial radio stations had broadcast some very successful art education programs for elementary kids. On the air, the instructor described various things and asked the kids to draw or paint what he had described. And each spring hundreds of children from all over the state came to the state capital to show off their artwork inspired by the radio programs.

Each picture was different. Each kid had interpreted the radio teacher's descriptions in a different way.

The programs were so successful that when television came along, the producers sought to transfer them to that medium. They were afraid of showing just a talking head on the screen however, so they had the instructor show the children some pictures of what he was poetically describing. They were meant to be just examples and "for instances."

But when the annual conclave of kid artists gathered that spring to show off their pictures, nearly all of them were almost exact copies of the pictures they had seen on the television programs.

The television version of the series was canceled the next year, and they went back to the radio programs. "Art requires imagination. Maybe religion does too," said Annie.

It was almost 9:00 p.m. by then, and Freddie and Bobby Joe headed back to the hotel, stopping for a burger on the way. When they got there, Freddie called the airline and was able to change their homeward-bound reservations to the first flight out the next morning. Then they left a 5:00 a.m. wake-up call with the front desk.

They checked out of the hotel just as dawn was breaking and grabbed a cab. Traffic was light, and they reached the airport around 6:30 a.m. But it wasn't until they were on board the plane that they both began to relax.

Freddie said that after his experience in New York, he was looking forward to getting home and hollering just a little bit at old Harrison Dillard who lived over on Elm Street. Harrison had a pet pig that he called Hammy Faye Bacon, who was constantly getting out of her pen and into Freddie's garden. He said the animal was supposedly the inspiration for that new country-western song "You Can't Help Being Ugly, but You Could Stay Home."

Bobby Joe said, "No—that song was inspired by the wife of a friend of mine." Freddie glanced over at this new young humorist with surprise and delight, and they both had a good laugh. They were pleased to be getting back to hayseed normal.

After they took off and were heading west, Freddie got to musing about the trip to New York and his busted dream. Somebody once said that you should be careful of what you wish for 'cause you might get it. And then he recalled that Irving Berlin had once penned a song that counseled "After You Get What You Want, You Don't Want It."

But as he thought it over, he came to agree—in a different way—with the title of the record he had played in the wee morning hours less than a week ago. "Yeah," he said to himself, "I guess the Lord must be in New York City. He's there 'cause He's needed there more than anywhere else."

And then he picked up the *New York Post* and began to read that morning's 9/11/01 edition.

Story 4

Too Fat for Paopao

What was he doing here! How had it come to this? Instead of spending the '60s reclining in a retirement chair in Florida, here he was swatting flies and quoting Bible verses in a sweltering hut in American Samoa!

The community *fale* (hut) was where distinguished guests were welcomed in an *'ava* ceremony. In spite of the fact that he had been taunted by the village children with his newly acquired nickname—Too Fat for *Paopao*—he was a privileged visitor. He sat awkwardly in his skirtlike *lava lava* (enough-enough) next to one of the wooden posts that supported the open-air structure. The spot was reserved for honored guests.

It was hot. The pandanus leaves that were woven into mats for sleeping and sitting were uncomfortable. His bulk and belly made any shifting difficult and threatened to reveal the purple shorts he wore under his native dress. And the cross-legged position made his old vein-popping legs ache.

His great girth, however, was an advantage here in Polynesia, where large men and women were admired, and truly large men with big stomachs were revered.

As the *palagi* (white man or foreign) chief, he was surrounded by the titled men of the village and his own retinue of two aides. He had given up trying to figure out the complex ranking of the assembled Samoans sitting around him on the floor of the fale.

But he and everyone else watched as a professional virgin created kava from the roots of a pepper plant. Perhaps she was *taupou*, the daughter of the village chief. When the concoction was ready, he raised the carved bowl, toasted everyone, and drank it in one gulp. It was of a muddy color and tasted bitter.

He had assumed such dignity as the occasion demanded, nodding appreciatively at the continued oratory of the High Talking Chief, even though he didn't understand most of it. His translator wasn't much help. The message was eloquent and full of flowery phrases in the formal Samoan language. He adopted a look of interest and understanding. At this level of the society, an apostolic countenance was mandatory.

As his mind drifted and he waited for the upcoming meal, he looked down at the garish, fringed souvenir pillows strewn about the fale. They had apparently been sent or brought back to the sleepy village by residents who had traveled to faraway climes.

In a mixture of lavender, red, gold, green, and blue, they spelled out "Love from San Diego" and "Portland—City of Roses." One, "Greetings from Greenwich," boggled the mind.

His gaze shifted outside the fale to the steaming rain forest and its drifting mists on one side, the palm-tree languor of the village on the other, and nearby, the trickling waterfall from the summit of the mountain, which (they said) was the highest in these coral-fringed islands. He was—he had to admit—in an Eden.

God seemed to be in this place. The word *Samoa* even meant "sacred center," according to some legends. Old *tusitalas* (storytellers) said that it is where the earth began, created by a god who caused the volcanoes to erupt from the ocean floor.

This American territory was indeed paradise—The Heart of the World. It lay some 2,600 miles southwest of Hawaii and 1,800 miles from New Zealand. Five islands and two coral atolls combined to make a total land area of only seventy-six square miles. But it was a land thick with orchids and fallen ginger blossoms on the jungle floor. Emerald green lagoons led out to coral reefs and the baby blue sea, while stunningly high cliffs overlooked undiscovered sugar-white beaches. The trees were heavy with papaya and mangoes.

But there was trouble in paradise. In spite of the natural beauty of the place, it had the look and air of abandonment for lack of interest. By American standards, the economy was in shambles. Only a small tuna canning factory and the local government provided any real employment for the roughly thirty thousand indigenous people with coconut skin the color of a smooth leather glove. A blue-eyed Samoan was about as rare as a naturally blond Chinese.

There was little tourism, the primitive coral roads were full of potholes, and even the government buildings in the little capital were shabby and nearly falling down. The only "hotel" was the rickety Rainmaker—a crumbling, former navy officers' club where blankets served as walls and big holes in the ceiling accommodated the daily rainfalls. It was a haven for cockroaches.

Neglect and decay were evident. Rusted vehicles abandoned after World War II had been used by the islanders and then left in the spot where they had died because no one could now get parts—even if they could figure out how to fix them. Piles of coconuts and empty cans were strewn around.

Although twice-weekly planes from the "outside world" and an occasional ship brought Western staples, foodstuffs, and kerosene—all of which the islanders had begun to rely on—the place was a mess, caught between Western civilization and native traditions. No one seemed to know or care about The Heart of Polynesia.

The Samoans operated at a casual pace, dictated by culture and climate. Work was usually done only when necessary. And although the trade winds offered respite, the constant heat sapped a person's energy. These congenial, happy people, who spoke a charming pidgin English, spent their days trapping fish, swimming, and lying in the shade in the midday sun. And at night they went to sleep, lulled by the sounds of tropical birds and the soft croaking of toads. It all fit the Samoan soul.

Their culture was a combination of Polynesian traditions and gods, and Christian piety. Missionaries had come to the islands in the late 1800s, bringing with them the certainty of salvation. Their message took. The excess of earlier days was tempered, and in spite of tawdry tales of lusty sailors and native girls, the islands became known by some as The Bible Belt of the South Pacific.

Although the Samoans were once fierce warriors, "civilization" had assuaged their combativeness. An exchange between two Samoans who had a fender bender with two beat-up old cars exemplified the "modern" Samoan.

One battered vehicle had an exhaust pipe held up by chicken wire and the key jammed forever into the ignition. The other clanked ominously and had a plastic sheet serving as a window on the front passenger's side and a rear door that was kept permanently shut by electrical tape. After the little collision, the two drivers emerged from their respective vehicles:

"Hey—whatsa matta you?"

"Whatsa matta ME?—whatsa matta YOU?"

"ME? YOU whatsa matta!"

This Samoan equanimity was due in large part to a society in which there were no truly big disasters and no real punishment. As Margaret Mead reported in her classic study of the place in the '20s (*Coming of Age in Samoa*), "No one plays for very high stakes."

The combination of Western culture, Christianity, and Polynesian traditions made for *fa'a Samoa*—the Samoan way. It was a unique manner of living. Contradictions abounded, and when modern thought clashed with the old native culture, the culture often won. The society was also bound together by a proud and strong oral tradition.

That tradition had carried over to the educational system. And it was there that the years of decay and neglect by the American government and the Samoan people were most noticeable.

The students came to school with an oral Samoan language that was inadequate for use as a base for further study. No clear curriculum objectives existed, and the teachers were poorly educated themselves. They failed to teach even the most fundamental of Western skills. The village school huts were overcrowded and dilapidated, and textbooks and other materials, if available, were hopelessly out of date and had little relevance to the experience or needs of the students.

As a result, the few students who managed to graduate from high school were at about the fourth-grade level in a mainland American school. There was little employment to be had, so many just drifted along in a torpid manner. The more ambitious males joined the American military and left the islands.

In spite of all this, some genius in the State Department back in Washington determined that this American territory was the ideal place to host a Pan Pacific conference on education, tropical agriculture, and economic development, with delegates from all the Pacific Rim countries. This same bureaucrat later confessed that he had never visited any of the tiny dots on the map way out in the vast Pacific, so a team hurriedly departed for American Samoa to assess the situation. Their report was scathing. And a *Reader's Digest* article called the islands "America's Slum in the South Pacific."

Something had to be done. The administration could not countenance hosting an international conference in such surroundings. Moreover, they needed to set an example of American know-how and benevolence, as well as exhibit a strong presence in the Pacific, which was a vital part of the Cold War strategy.

So the U.S. president appointed a far-seeing palagi governor to the job in American Samoa. In a series of emergency meetings back in Washington, this new administrator focused on the need to restructure the educational system, both as a humanitarian and political necessity.

Someone in the White House had the good sense to contact the National Association of Educational Broadcasters (NAEB) and its director of Research and Development. Although he wasn't known then as Too Fat for Paopao, this man and his staff had written a paper for the administration, citing the potential use of television as an integral part of the day-to-day instructional process—particularly in developing countries.

And so he—"himself," as he often called himself—was called in to develop a comprehensive plan to completely redo the educational system of American Samoa. In the do-your-own-thing culture of the day on the mainland, he found himself convening curriculum specialists who seemed to be trying to dress like their children. But now his rumpled self did not cotton to the overseeing government officials, whose sole purpose seemed to be to show off clothing that did not wrinkle when you sat down.

He had been reluctant at first. And now here he was—on site—trying to get all the pieces together to implement the plan. The system he and his staff had designed called for the support of, rather than replacement of, the native teachers, who in a cooperative, instructional manner would make optimum use of television. The objective was to make the Samoan kids bilingual and academically competitive in the world market.

A team of support personnel would devise daily lessons presented by on-air teachers for transmittal to the village schools. Those schools would be completely rebuilt and television receivers installed. The students would learn rather than just be taught. And the village teachers would learn in the process too.

To the palagi chief this was the dream of a lifetime. Here was a chance to test all of the educational theories he and his colleagues had developed over the years. Television would be used not as a supplementary enriching adjunct, but as a primary and integral part of the instructional process.

Enabling all of this to happen required a massive influx of funds. Fourteen million dollars was initially allocated to build six channels of broadcast television from ten videotape recorders, four fully equipped studios, and two-way radio systems connecting every school to the educational center in the capital at Pago Pago for immediate feedback. Preliminary construction began, and technicians, directors, curriculum specialists, artists, researchers, and on-air teachers were hired in the United States and trained to implement the newly written curriculum.

It was a gigantic task. Very few Samoans had ever seen television. It was going to be a massive undertaking! And like all revolutionary projects, it was not without controversy in a society where change came ever so slowly. Some of the local village chiefs viewed the project as an assault on the easy Samoan way of life. "Why not we jest go long da way we hav an eat our breadfruit inda shade?" they asked. Besides, comprehending new ideas was a strenuous business.

Others resented any possible erosion of their authority. They were suspicious of anyone or anything that held so much power. And they seemed to agree with that old Presbyterian dictum that progress was all right as long as it didn't change anything. The Samoan tradition of *musu* (unwillingness toward any course of action) permeated every aspect of the Samoan society.

One of the most vocal examples of this obstinacy was Chief Tuiasasopo, on one of the outlying islands. He was one of the paramount chiefs, and his big bulk was now sitting comfortably across from the palagi chief in an equally honored spot in the fale. His large High Talking Chief and his retinue of titled nobility were to his side and behind him. The village the chief oversaw was one of the most isolated in a remote land in the middle of nowhere. It was some sixty miles from Pago Pago, and this was the palagi chief's second attempt at a long *malaga* (journey) to see the obstinate chief.

The palagi chief was, if anything, persistent. For in spite of the fact that the governor's edict made adherence to the new education system mandatory, it was prudent to try to elicit cooperation from all segments of the society and, most importantly, from the village chiefs.

In the first attempt, the palagi chief and his two aides—a Samoan interpreter and a stateside assistant—had set sail in a rusted LST (Landing Ship Tank) left over from World War II. His goal was to persuade the reluctant chief of the values of this new method of education. He was looking forward to what he hoped would not be a confrontation but rather—as he put it—a "CAREfrontation."

The let-down front of the vessel they boarded had been welded shut and a rotting wooden deck supported the passengers and cargo. Chains and the anchor were rusted to the point of disintegration, and there were bullet holes in the starboard side. The thing did not look seaworthy. It traveled about five miles an hour. But it was fondly called The Samoan Navy.

The propellers of the vessel were off-kilter somehow, which made it shake from side to side. The cargo—canned tuna, vegetables, Kool-Aid, Spam, Ketchup, and Jell-O, along with cigarettes and diapers and iced tea—was piled on the deck in no particular order. But as they got under way, the passengers marveled at the beauty around them under the tropical sun. The trade-wind clouds hung over the vessel like soft pillows. The parade of tropical fish in the crystal clear blue waters, the turquoise-shaded coves, and the inviting beaches were mesmerizing.

Still, it was a long, nasty trip. They sailed through a few squalls, which left the fresh air perfumed by plumeria and bougainvillea. When they arrived at the island, the captain of the vessel put aside his pipe long enough to anchor outside the reef and wait for the transportation that was to take the party ashore and to the village. The obstreperous village chief had sent out a large outrigger with two native paddlers who pulled up alongside the LST and prepared to take the three passengers to

shore—one at a time. The ranking member—the palagi chief—
was to be first.

But in an attempt to "relate" to fa'a Samoa, he waved the outrigger off and hollered to an accompanying one-man paopao to
come alongside. He would paddle himself to shore!

The lad in the tiny outrigger pulled up beside the LST and
slipped overboard, holding the small craft next to a little platform at the side of the bigger vessel. The small stepping place was
at the end of a fraying rope ladder.

The palagi chief descended that ladder with as much dignity
as he could muster, his big body moving with crablike caution.
When he reached the platform just above the water, he paused to
get his balance in the gentle waves that swayed both vessels.
Then he stepped precariously—one foot at a time—into the center of the little outrigger. There he stood upright—smiling and
completely in command of the situation—an admiral surveying
his soon-to-be domain.

But as he lowered himself majestically onto the small seat and
reached for the paddle, the little craft began to sink. Slowly,
surely, the tiny outrigger began to disappear into the water!

It was as if the giant hand of God had come down on his head
and was pushing him and the paopao, gradually but inexorably,
downward. In ten seconds the little outrigger simply disappeared,
leaving behind an incredulous dignitary!

A look of astonishment overcame the face of the vessel's original occupant, dog-paddling alongside the bigger ship. Onlookers
on the beach, on the surrounding outriggers, and on the LST were
equally dumbfounded. They exchanged glances as if to say, Did
you see what I saw?

There was nothing anyone could do. It had happened so
fast. One of the crew unleashed a big rubber truck tire that was

used as a bumper and threw it overboard, hitting the palagi chief on the head, momentarily stunning him. Another crew member clambered down the ladder and pulled the floundering dignitary to safety on the little platform. It was like beaching a whale.

After a minute or two, the dripping palagi chief climbed laboriously up the ladder to the comforting rust bucket of a vessel. Everyone breathed a sigh of relief.

The only real casualty of the affair was his straw hat, which had floated out to sea. It was never recovered, so the villagers viewed it as a divine message that the god of the sea had evidently needed some shade for his head.

Any further attempts to land passengers or cargo that day were abandoned, and the LST began its ten-hour return to Pago Pago. When they got there, the palagi chief was greeted with the taunts of the native children who swarmed down to meet them.

"Too Fat for Paopao!" they chanted as they skipped around him. The coconut wireless had done its job.

The palagi chief was too stubborn to cancel the visit to the chief in the outer island and rescheduled it for the next week. But he came down with one of his periodic illnesses and had to take to his bed, leaving for a time the cajoling, ordering, teaching, and ministering to the growing number of the project's stateside and native personnel. The delay did give his new staff a time to reflect on their boss.

"Himself" was bigger than life—both in physical size and intellect. It was as if a combination of Churchill, Ben Franklin, and Santa Claus had somehow deigned to hire them!

His 240 pounds were spread over a sturdy trunk supported by thighs and large-veined calves, but his real heftiness had come with age and was concentrated in a big belly. His whole structure was topped off by a leonine head that featured a broad, once-broken nose, blue eyes, and thinning hair. Age spots dotted his massive hands.

But his face was truly the most fascinating thing about him. It ran the gauntlet of his every emotion—loving, pouting, disconsolate, joyous, depressed—depending on the day and circumstances. He was alternately proud, grouchy, arrogant, bored, gleeful—an ever-changing kaleidoscope of moods.

In spite of nearly constant pain from an old back injury, many other maladies, and the artificial stomach he harbored, he viewed life as a sort of wondrous pageant. And he, of course, was at center stage under a brilliant spotlight.

For he tended to dominate everything—a conversation, a meeting, a conference table. He appeared to have an interior vision of the world that God required him to share. Fortunately, his rhetoric was almost always equal to the task, and his baritone rumbled along with ideas of astonishing clarity. Sometimes even he seemed astonished by his oratory. And it was easier for him to APPEAR humble than to BE so.

He was, EVERYONE ON HIS NEW STAFF AGREED, ONE OF THE WORLD'S GREAT ORIGINALS—A MAN LIKE FEW OTHERS.

He seemed to revel in the fact that he was a self-made man, thus saving God (he chuckled) from an awful responsibility. He was like the philosopher Rasselas, who watched the sun rise for years and finally concluded that it rose only because he was watching.

He believed strongly in the virtues of diligence and industry—and opportunity for all. His credo was to promote a social order that lifted the common man so he could work toward the common good. And he believed that one could best serve God by serving one another.

Still, he was repeatedly dismayed at the wilderness of the human heart. His most damaging words were often soft and tinged with resignation. "The spirit of decency does not abide in you," was his despondent mutter one day to a colleague who had betrayed him.

That sentiment often carried over to other aspects of his life. He was seen to sniffle over a little girl's gift of a garland, made from the blossoms of the *pua* tree, and a manly handshake from a native boy would unleash a misting of the eyes. He was unabashed in displaying this soft part of himself. Perhaps it was an actor's inborn sentimentality. Perhaps the moments were reminders of a wished-for childhood purity. Perhaps his emotions were so close to the surface that they occasionally bubbled over when loving thoughts intruded.

He was, everyone on his new staff agreed, one of the world's great originals—a man like few others.

He had experienced a hardscrabble beginning. Born one minute before the turn of the century, he said he always felt like he was behind. His hard-drinking father was a construction superintendent who dragged mother and child along from project to project throughout the South. His mother, however, was a God-fearing Baptist, full of a love for the Lord. She instilled in him a respect for and knowledge of the Bible. He was forced to memorize many passages, for she maintained, "They were God's Word."

So hours were spent in the study of the Good Book, in drawing rooms and parlors, waiting for his father to come home. And he and his mother attended church as regularly as possible.

His schooling was erratic because of all the travel, but he was brilliant in the classroom and on the playground. Always the "new kid," he fought off bullies and was tagged with the nickname Turk. He somehow managed to graduate from high school and fought in the trenches in World War I. He later did a stint as a prizefighter and drove a taxi in Manhattan, then pursued a career on the B. F. Keith Vaudeville circuit. As the understudy of "The Man of a Thousand Bible Passages," he used his childhood lessons as a base for increasing his memorization of the Bible.

Somewhere along the line he also acquired a couple of degrees, taught in both high school and college, and became a vocational education administrator. He later pioneered in educational television, constructing one of the nation's first stations. Still later he became an internationally known expert and consultant to foreign governments on the use of technology in education. He saw its potential as a teaching tool. And it was in this capacity that he was in American Samoa.

So here he was, facing one of his biggest challenges and the opportunity to put his educational theories to a real test. Nothing would stand in the way, even though some of his colleagues considered it an "insurmountable opportunity." But it was his dream, and he was full of passion for it. In spite of his catalog of infirmities, he would see it through to a glorious conclusion.

So after he had recovered from his illness, the palagi chief and his two staff members set out once again to the outlying island and its recalcitrant chief. He was looking forward to the meeting, where he was sure his formidable verbal powers would rule the day.

This time his staff had persuaded the captain of the LST to sail around the island to a small, banjo-shaped harbor on the leeward side. It had a little abandoned wharf jutting out in the water. There was no village or people, but they could tie up there and avoid the outrigger rides.

All went as planned, and they were met by an old Jeep and a young driver who was to take them around and over the big mountain to the stubborn chief's village for a second try at a meeting.

At the driver's urging, they strapped themselves in, using the makeshift seat belts cut out of old inner tubes, and began the bouncing, bone-shaking trip over a trail hacked out of the jungle.

Soon they were in another world—a world of green light filtered through the trees that hung over the sides of the narrow road that consisted of loose gravel and muddy ruts. The young driver seemed to take pleasure in steering directly at the many potholes. Ferns brushed their foreheads, and they spent a lot of time ducking.

When the group finally arrived at the village, they were met by the children who surrounded the old jeep with welcoming shouts of *Talofa* (hello) and chants of Too Fat for Paopao.

And now as they sat in the community fale, they listened to the High Talking Chief. After his warming-up soliloquy about the loveliness of Samoa, the love of the Samoans for the Americans, and the love of everyone for everyone in the world (all in formal Samoan), he moved toward the point of all of his oratory. As the diplomat and negotiator, he had the duty to present the chief's position on any matter. Although the *matai* (headmen) herein assembled were consulted in this society of social status, the final decision and any action was the chief's.

The High Talking Chief began to shorten his sentences, directly addressing Too Fat for Paopao in broken English. "We admire you love of fa'a Samoa," he said, using broad gestures to emphasize his points. "You make us happy with embraces of our *aiga* (family). Our *matua* (parents) want children to live-love under beeg skies of beloved land all round. We believeve our *a'oga* (school) and *faia'oga* (teacher) good. Our *fale'oga* (schoolhouse) good. So why we try sumtink else?" continued the High Talking Chief. "Why we tink too much? Our land no bigga than fly in beeg world. But here is silence. Here is peace. Here is"—and he paused, summoning up the word—"SERENE! We are generouses peeple—kind—slow. Come liff wit us. Join our aiga. I will be your brudda. Here you live like child—simple. Here you hunt land crabs in moonlight. Here you go torch fishin'. Here you rest in cool shade of paradises. Here you live in love. Here you die in peace. An' bye an' bye—when you gunna gimme Jackie Kennedy's phone number?"

Having made his case, the High Talking Chief sat down, and the meal was served. There were large banana-leaf platters of burned chicken, roasted pig, and fresh fish, all accompanied by papaya and mango and breadfruit. It was a feast.

All through the welcoming speeches and the meal, the chief and Too Fat for Paopao had been smiling and nodding and eying one another warily. The chief was in his sixties and plump with Polynesian royalty, topping the scales at more than three hundred pounds.

Along with many other large Samoans, he didn't seem to think he had done it to himself. He had an air about him and a triple chin that seemed to say, "Look what happened to me!" A devout Christian, he looked forward to testing his beliefs and will against the palagi chief.

During the meal, each man attempted to somehow take the measure of the other by a gesture, a look, or an attitude. Both realized that this was a significant meeting. A lot was at stake. Two bigger-than-life leaders were going to decide the fate of a lot of people on this little island.

Now that the chief's position had been explained so eloquently by the High Talking Chief and the meal was over, it was the palagi chief's turn. The fire was on his side, as they said in the tropics. He glanced at his interpreter, cleared his throat, and began. There was silence in the fale.

He spoke of the love of America for its far-flung brothers here in the Pacific. He spoke of the beauty of the land and the waters. He spoke of the respect all held for fa'a Samoa.

"But," he said, "it is imperative that the Samoan people learn to live in the world society. Modern transportation and communication are bringing the world to the islands, whether you want it or not. You can no longer live in beautiful isolation.

"While you must always revere and honor the gods of the old days and the God of the new days, the people must learn to accept the new ways," he continued. "You must keep your own culture, but also take advantage of all that is offered to improve your lives.

"The children must be educated to be able to take their place both in the big world and here in Samoa. They must learn new ways and language in order to make a finer society. They will lead the Samoan people to better days in the future.

"The rewards will be good health care for all of the people, more food and clothing, and better housing," he said. "The villages will be cleaner, the roads will be improved, and more people will come to visit these beautiful islands. There will be more jobs for everyone, even in this village. The people will prosper and be happier, and everyone will sing and dance."

Looking directly into the chief's eyes, he appealed to the man's sense of duty. "You must take the leadership in this new way, or history will never forgive you," he intoned passionately. And with that he sat back, confident that his case had been made.

The translator finished his work. And then, for the first time in the meeting, the chief spoke. Eying his rival, he asked in broken English, "So—you like 'em historee?"

The palagi chief nodded.

"Den you tell me. Who president in 1829?" the chief asked in his deep bass voice.

Too Fat for Paopao was stunned. What was this all about? Ah—yes—a test.

Okay, let's see, he thought. *I'll take that challenge and do him one better.* Ransacking his memory, he finally came up with an answer he hoped was right. "Andy Jackson," he said.

A nod from the chief told him he was on target and emboldened him to ask a return question. "Who was president in 1861?" he queried.

"Abraham Lincoln, who freed the slaves," the Samoan chief answered. "Who follow him?"

There was a pause as his Caucasian opponent scratched his head. Finally it came to him. "Andrew Johnson!" A smile was his reward. But this was getting tough. *How far can we go with this,* the palagi chief wondered to himself as he formulated another question. "Who was President in 1909?"

"William Howard Taft," said the chief promptly.

Where did this guy get this kind of information? Too Fat for Paopao looked over at his interpreter, who mouthed the word *missionaries.* And the contest was on.

"Who president in 1845?" asked the chief.

Too Fat for Paopao was stymied.

"James Knox Polk," said the chief, answering his own question.

It was the palagi chief's turn. He tried to stick to the twentieth century, for there he had at least a fighting chance. "Theodore Roosevelt?" he questioned.

"1901 to 1909," said the chief without hesitation.

But the village leader was not having any of these modern guys, and it was his turn. "Grover Cleveland?" he asked his opponent.

The palagi chief shook his head.

"Rutherford Birchard Hayes?"

A hopeless and despondent shrug was the response.

Finally, as if to give Too Fat for Paopao a chance, the chief offered up, "Herbert Clark Hoover?"

"1929 to 1932," shouted the palagi chief triumphantly!

But he and everyone else knew he had lost this scrimmage. And in the polite kindness that was so much a part of the culture, the chief motioned to a waiting group of children, who lined up and presented the dignitaries with a song in honor of the occasion.

It was a welcome respite for Too Fat for Paopao. The Samoan song was beautiful and soothing, and he misted over. He realized that he had lost this round but would recover. He would prevail, he told himself. But just as he regained his equilibrium, he found that he was to be tested again.

Perhaps inspired by the music, the chief asked the palagi chief to honor *them* with a song! Oh my! He was no singer. But this was now becoming a contest between him and the chief. He could hardly refuse.

The only thing that popped into his mind was a ballad from the 1930s. As Charles Ives once reminded everyone, "There is a place in the heart where old songs dwell." So, inspired by the setting, Too Fat for Paopao slowly lumbered to his feet and, swaying slightly, began the lyrics to "Deep Purple" in a voice that should never have made it out of the shower.

> *When the deep purple falls, over sleepy garden walls,*
> *and the sun begins to linger in the sky—*

But at this point his memory faded, and he had to finish the song with a lot of "la la las." Still, it was greeted with raucous cheers from the assemblage in the fale.

"Your turn," said the palagi chief, gesturing politely to his counterpart as he collapsed into his former position.

The Samoan chief hesitated, as if gathering his thoughts, and then struggled to his feet, rearranging his lava lava. There in the sweltering heat of the tropics, amidst the flies and remains of the feast, he straightened up to military attention, and his rumbling bass sang out proudly, proclaiming with great vigor:

> *There is no place like Nebraska, dear old Nebraska U.*
> *Where the girls are the fairest, the boys are the squarest*
> *Of any old place that we knew.*
> *There is no place like Nebraska, where we're all true blue*
> *We all stick together in all kinds of weather,*
> *At dear old Nebraska U!*

The cheers filled the early night. The palagi chief was robbed of his speech. He sat there, mouth agape—his brain working frantically. Finally he looked over at his translator, who once again mouthed *missionaries*.

When he gathered his senses, he knew this second round of the contest between him and the chief was over. He could never top a rendition of a University of Nebraska fight song by a massive, half-naked Samoan chief in the middle of the Pacific Ocean. He smiled, acknowledging his surrender with a little half bow.

There was a pause in the proceedings. Dusk was upon them, and torches were being lit. It was a time for reflection.

This encounter was not going well. Too Fat for Paopao was losing face and position. He had lost two rounds. Desperate to find something he could excel in, he glanced once again around the fale. Two of the matai had left, and their absence revealed a startling new sight.

Behind where they had sat, on a little old red Radio Flyer wagon, lay an enormous open Bible—six inches thick. Evidently the Word of God was thus movable and could be wheeled wherever the chief went.

A glance over at his interpreter confirmed the notion that

both had once been gifts of the missionaries—probably when the chief was young. Here was his angle.

Here was his way to persuade the chief of his position and convince him to support the new educational system and its television component. Besides, he had the authority of the territorial governor on his side. He could use that.

He would call on his stint in vaudeville and his Baptist upbringing, which had given him a knowledge of the Bible so long ago. He hoped his memory would be up to it. He hoped his recall of biblical passages had not been eroded by decades of other thoughts and by the intrusion of more immediate concerns. It was worth a try.

So, seeking to impress and gain the village leader's confidence, he redirected his attention to the chief. Capitalizing on the authority of the territorial governor, he summoned up a phrase from the Good Book. "Let every soul be subject unto the higher powers," he said sternly.

The chief had been briefly napping (or perhaps praying with his eyes closed) but straightened up at the sound of the Bible verse. Shaking his head to clear his thoughts, he responded in a soothing and gentle voice: "We ought to obey God rather than men."

Oh my, thought the palagi chief, *another contest. Okay, I'll see you one and raise you one.* "Submit yourselves to every ordinance of man for the Lord's sake."

"Owe no man any thing, but to love one another: for he that loveth another hath fulfilled the law," responded the chief in an unperturbed way. And, evidently attempting to get to the heart of the matter by questioning the origins and legitimacy of the new educational television system, he continued: "Who shall go over the sea for us, and bring it unto us, that we may hear it, and do it?" He sat back and waited for an answer.

"The doers of the law shall be justified," answered the palagi chief. And he sat back.

"But that no man is justified by the law in the sight of God," countered the host chief.

They were at a temporary stalemate. To break the tension, the Samoan chief silently lifted his glass in tribute to his opponent.

As he raised his glass in return, the palagi chief smiled back and said, "And lead us not into temptation."

"My brethren, count it all joy when ye fall into divers temptations," countered the Samoan chief.

They both burst into laughter. And those around them who had been watching with a collective frozen smile on their faces, while listening to the tennislike exchanges, also laughed with relief. The two combatants studied one another with new respect.

Too Fat for Paopao had begun to suffer from the hiccups, and it was embarrassing. As he fought to overcome the spasms, a sentence from *The Merchant of Venice* came to his mind. "The Devil can cite scripture for his purpose." Weren't they both referencing the Scriptures, each for his own purpose? Weren't they making their points with biblical passages that appeared to be contrary? Weren't they being devils?

Shrugging off those thoughts, Too Fat for Paopao decided to take another tack. He would appeal to the chief's respect for the Good Book and learning and his fun-loving nature. So he searched the vagaries of his memory and resumed the contest with "Happy is the man that findeth wisdom, and the man that getteth understanding."

"Hath not God made foolish the wisdom of this world?" countered the chief.

But the palagi chief was not giving up. "Wisdom is the principal thing; therefore get wisdom; and with all thy getting get understanding."

The chief answered softly, "For in much wisdom is much grief: and he that increaseth knowledge increaseth sorrow."

They seemed to once again be at loggerheads.

But the Samoan chief was compassionate and kind. He sought to accommodate and flatter the palagi chief while imparting a caution. "You, beeg mon. You important mon. You believe in *Atua* (God). You have done many tings." But he raised a finger— "For by grace are ye saved through faith: . . . it is the gift of God, not of works."

Too Fat for Paopao flushed but felt compelled to counter the thought. Rummaging through his memory, he came up with "By works a man is justified, and not by faith only." It was one of his favorite biblical passages that he hadn't thought about in years.

"No, no," exclaimed the chief. "Take heed . . . do not sound a trumpet before thee."

The palagi chief struggled with the crisscrosses of his memory to find the passage that would apparently counter that thought. It was elusive—just out of reach. But from the deep recesses of his mind, it finally burst forth in "Let your light so shine before men, that they may see your good works, and glorify your Father which is in heaven."

He breathed a sigh of relief. But by now his brain was getting tired of all the concentration, and he feared his memory would falter. So he sought to change the emphasis. It was getting late, and there was no way they could return to Pago Pago that night. But perhaps he could appeal to the chief's responsibility for his aiga and the Polynesian love of kids—and bring the contest to an end.

Samoan children were raised in a culture that featured the warm circle of a large homogenous family. They were looked after by a veritable army of caring adults. But the current schools did not reward the bright or punish the slow. All were treated alike. It virtually guaranteed a stifling mediocrity.

So he set out a warning. The children of the village would suffer in the big world, he said, unless the chief adopted the new form of education. Sifting through his mind he came up with a suitable verse: "For I the LORD thy God am a jealous God, visiting the iniquity of the fathers upon the children."

"The son shall NOT bear the iniquity of the father," replied the chief firmly.

And the two looked at one another in a silence that reflected profound respect. They were both good students of the Bible and its seeming contradictions.

Finally the chief spoke. "You good mon. You *Kerisiano* (Christian). I like this battle. But enof." He smiled in an almost beatific manner as he sought to bring the meeting to a close with a lighthearted sally at his opponent. "Answer a fool according to his folly, lest he be wise in his own conceit."

But Too Fat for Paopao had the last word. "Answer NOT a fool according to his folly, lest thou also be like unto him."

The Samoan chief roared with laughter. And he brought the meeting to a close. "Mo bettah we do your way, Mistah Televisson. Is good for chil'ren. Is good for us." And turning to the assembled elders, he proclaimed, "Behold, how good and how pleasant it is for brethren to dwell together in unity!"

Everybody clapped.

The palagi chief sighed with relief. He had held his own in the most important of the verbal contests. The paramount chief would support the endeavor if only because, in the Samoan tradition, he was avoiding a difficult situation and continued conflict.

As the meeting broke up, Too Fat for Paopao reclined in the fale on a purple pillow that promised him "Love from Pittsburgh."

And he slept soundly, in spite of a barking dog that kept everyone else awake. Or so the natives in Pago Pago heard, after the coconut wireless had once again done its job.

The next morning, the palagis were awakened by a lavender dawn and the joyous shouts of children at play. And after a breakfast of breadfruit, Cheerios drowned in water, and that once-a-year seafood delicacy *palolo*, they began their trip back over the mountain to the wharf and the LST, which would take them back to Pago Pago.

This time they rode in a little Datsun bus, with some of the villagers and the chief. The trip was less strenuous, for the conveyance had some rusted, but workable, springs, and they were spared the ducking to avoid the branches of the jungle. Once back at the ship, as they waited for the captain and his crew to cast off, they admired the beauty of the lush island and thought of the gentleness of its inhabitants, who proved there was a God. When the boat pulled away from the dock, they waved and shouted *"Tofa soifua!"* (good-bye; good health) and *"Fa'afetai!"* (thank you).

And Too Fat for Paopao mumbled out of the corner of his mouth to his aides, "If we are going to do any more of these, get me a history of the United States and a Bible for my night-stand."

A Postscript

Any true evaluation of the success of the new educational system in American Samoa was planned to take at least twelve years, when the first class taught had completed the twelfth grade. After four years, test results and other measures indicated that the system was on track in improving the teaching and learning of the Samoan children. It was gaining an international reputation in educational circles.

But a newly appointed governor was determined that he would directly control and manage the educational system and its television component. The NAEB chose not to renew its contract to oversee the endeavor, and it was gradually abandoned by the territorial government.

What Margaret Mead wrote in the '20s applied to the '60s. "The Samoans have only taken such parts of our culture that made their life more comfortable, their culture more flexible." In the end, it was a struggle between the dreams of Too Fat for Paopao and reality—and reality won.

In later years he spoke of the experience and the Samoan people with a quote from Psalm 55:14: "We took sweet counsel together."

The
Great
Episcopalian
Bear Hunt

Featherstone's dander was up, albeit in a gentlemanly manner. On a bright day, when big clouds sailed along on a light breeze, he learned that his nemesis had managed to outmaneuver him. In Featherstone's absence, Warren E. Radcliff had persuaded the Vestry—the local governing board of the church—to authorize a crazy idea as a fund-raiser!

They were to have a Bear Barbecue in the parking lot on the grounds on the twenty-third of next month, to raise money for a new roof for the sanctuary. A Bear Barbecue, of all things! Preceded by a Bear Hunt! By church members! It was most unseemly!

The Church of the Heavenly Rest of Carlson, Iowa, was Featherstone's domain. It was Episcopal. As Senior Warden of the Vestry, he presided over the activities of the church in a lordly manner befitting his station. He kept a tight rein on the budget, made sure no incompetent ne'er-do-well was hired as sexton and chief caretaker of the place, and watched out for any strange fund-raising proposals from Radcliff.

But now one had slipped past him. While Featherstone was unavoidably absent from the monthly meeting, the Junior Warden had allowed Radcliff's idea about bears to be presented to the Vestry. And they had bought it!

As Harvey bicycled to the little church for a meeting with Father Conklin, he despaired. Throughout the years, the church had struggled to find ways of turning a buck for a good cause. The ladies had often launched a bazaar and rummage sale, but the proceeds from that event went directly to them and their philanthropies. The youth group's annual car-wash profit was dedicated to their use. The ladies did try a craft fair to benefit the whole church, but with the exception of Mrs. Worthington's sachets and Mrs. Castle's dried wreaths, the parishioners' crafts weren't very good and didn't sell well at all. Some were so terrible they seemed inspired. And a pancake breakfast had been a flop.

Featherstone had himself promoted the holding of croquet matches in the cloister last summer. Admission was charged, and the ladies had a stand with little cucumber sandwiches, strawberries with cream, and punch for sale.

The contestants were all in white and wore straw hats, and many of the ladies in attendance were resplendent in pastel gowns and hats as big as the tire on a car. It started out as a wonderfully delightful garden party. But no one had counted on the competitiveness of the Episcopal men of the Hawkeye state.

As the afternoon wore on, unexpected mutterings began to be heard. Wives began to take sides and root for their husbands in a decidedly unladylike manner. When one aggressive player knocked his opponent's ball off court, Featherstone actually had to step in and separate the two. By this time, bets were being made on the sidelines, a fistfight had started up near the food stand, and a little kid got trampled in the crowd. Finally the priest stepped in and calmed everybody down with a prayer before canceling the contests.

The matches hadn't raised much money. Few of Carlson's other citizens had showed up, since they had deemed it a rather snooty sport played by a bunch of snooty people.

So no more Killer Croquet. But bears? A barbecue? Featherstone shook his head as he pedaled along. *Radcliff deserves a good talking to.*

By the time he got to the church, however, he had begun to calm down a bit. At last he was safe, on familiar ground. The brick edifice, with its vines and Norman-like bell tower, sat on a little hill in the northern part of town. God's Little Acre, they called it. The Agnus Dei was carved above the door. Inside it was cool and dark and quiet and somewhat damp. He could see the altar, font, and Jacobean pulpit, as well as the stained-glass

windows that let in just enough light to form slanting shadows through the beams above.

The rector was waiting in his study, dressed in his working uniform of gray slacks, gray jacket, black shirt, and white clerical collar.

"Isn't there something we can do about this debacle?" asked Featherstone.

"Alas," said Father Conklin, "it's all been decided. It's too late, I'm afraid."

"But we're Episcopalian! This simply won't do!"

The priest shook his head dolefully and stretched out his hands in a helpless gesture.

"But this is Iowa," pleaded Featherstone. "What do Iowans know about bears, for heaven's sake? Let alone hunting them and eating them!"

The priest listened half-heartedly to Harvey Featherstone's rantings. He even cast his eyes downward with a look that carried with it (he hoped) a hint of regretful remorse.

But he was, in fact, secretly pleased that the Vestry had approved the event. They needed some get-up-and-go ideas— even as crazy as this one sounded—to change and broaden the image of the church. And, Lord knows, they needed the money!

The roof was in sad shape. Three leaks had appeared recently in the section above his study, staining its dark woodwork and dripping onto the brass lamps with the green shades. But the patch was only a temporary measure.

Besides, they were really in the doldrums. The parish was mirroring the times. Everything—and everybody—was wafting along in the afterglow of World War II, delighted with all the new consumer items available, like Tupperware and cake mixes and aluminum foil.

Folks were downright respectful and virtuous. It was rather easy to be so in Iowa, where there was little to lead one into temptation. Virtue came easily to folks who would rather do the right thing than engage in all the energy and stress that vice could bring. It really took some effort to get into trouble, and at the heart of it all, the parishioners of the Church of the Heavenly Rest were usually just too lazy to commit much sin.

This attitude had begun to carry over to the rector. He had little to challenge him these days except the fund-raising problem. Oh, there had been the croquet matches, and there was Mrs. Day, the plump lady congregant who kept insisting that she be allowed to whistle her love for Christ during the Eucharist. She thought "Rock of Ages" would be appropriate. Mrs. Day was a convert from a Fundamentalist church and wore gobs of makeup, as if she needed to look extra nice if the good Lord suddenly decided to take her away.

And there was her "friend," Mrs. Worthington, whose sister was a member of a militant wing of the Salvation Army in nearby Sioux City and who (some said) wore "aggressive underwear." Mrs. Worthington had whispered to him that if Mrs. Day was allowed to do her whistling, then she wanted to do her modern dance interpretation of "Onward Christian Soldiers" after the consecration of the Elements.

And he had been forced to deal with the two amorous high-school kids whom he had caught necking in a dark corner of the nave. They were Presbyterians. When he advised them that they were "not welcome here doing that," the lad had sighed and said, "That's what they said at the grocery store!"

Otherwise, things at the church and the rectory seemed to move along at a glacial pace. His wife was a steady companion, his kids were well-behaved, and things were—well—just a bit dull. This bear thing might jog him and his parishioners out of their lethargy and make them not seem so stuck-up in the eyes of the community. Maybe it would stop some people around town from calling their place of worship the Church of the Heavenly Dressed.

After all, it was a lot less daft than some of Warren Radcliff's previous fund-raising ideas. Most of them were decidedly out of the ordinary, even though he kept submitting them, to the consternation of Featherstone and the Vestry.

There was his proposal for an International Chicken Flying Meet. All you needed, Radcliff said, were some farm folk who had confidence in their fowls' ability to fly a bit, a ten-foot platform to serve as a launching pad, and a toilet plunger to give the birds a

gentle prod. The local members of the Humane Society could supervise things so that no chicken got hurt, and the one that flew the farthest would win. In addition to the entry fees, the church could set up some bleachers and charge admission for the contest and for the chicken dinner afterward.

When that one didn't fly, Radcliff came up with a proposal for a Jump for Jesus Jamboree. They'd set up some trampolines and . . .

Featherstone had also shot that one down. But Radcliff was undeterred. The Idea Man kept trying and eventually came up with the bear scheme. And he proposed it on the day he knew Featherstone would be away.

What they'd do, Radcliff said, was this: He and two other parishioners would go on a hunting trip to Canada to shoot some bears. They would pay their own way, so there would be no expenses for the expedition. The guys would take along a battery-operated wire recorder that Radcliff had liberated from his service days in World War II and talk into it about their hunt and the progress they were making. They'd phone home periodically, and the recording would be played back over the local radio station, where Radcliff had an "in" with the management.

This would build up excitement and promote the big event! Since practically nobody in town had ever tasted bear meat, people would turn out and pay for the exotic-tasting bruin sandwiches (with coleslaw and potato chips and a beverage). They'd hold the event on a Sunday afternoon in the church parking lot and have a band for entertainment.

He mentioned that Parker Wheatly would be one of the hunters and that "two or three other guys were interested."

Wheatly was a longtime member of the congregation and a gentle sportsman, so his participation probably persuaded at least some members of the Vestry to go along with the plan, even if Radcliff *was* a little balmy. People in the church and around town generally agreed that he marched to his own drum and bugle corps.

This was unusual in a little village in a state in the middle of everywhere, where the lifestyle of its citizens—economically, politically, socially—mirrored its geography. The folks of Hawkeyeland had never taken much to excess. Moderation was then—and is now—the key to everything. A visitor from abroad had once called the state the most American part of America.

So Radcliff's wacky proposals, somewhere out there amidst the amber waves of grain in northwest Iowa, were unusual. In a place where the cornfields ran smack up against the rolling greens at the Carlson Country Club and farmers lived poor but died rich, Radcliff stood out. He had once pointed out to the Vestry that if the letters in "Episcopal" were rearranged, they could spell "Pepsi Cola."

The Idea Man had been a resident of Carlson now for about seven years. The town was large enough—some 9,200 souls— to be able to support two newspapers and a radio station. There was KHEJ, the daily *Times*, and the weekly *Courier*. Radcliff was editor of the latter. The newspapers were both owned by the same family and one of Radcliff's friends owned the radio station.

He had moved into the job from his position as the owner-editor of a little weekly paper in a nearby town that he and another veteran had started up after World War II. They had gone broke, however, for they didn't realize that some places are too small to support even a weekly rag.

Once in his new job in the larger town, Radcliff set out to improve the *Courier* and to increase its ads. In a takeoff of the famous slogan of the *New York Times*, he put his own motto on the masthead: *All the News That Fits, We Print*

Some subscribers saw a liberal implication in the slogan, for Radcliff really didn't try to hide his membership in the Democrat party. And in a Republican enclave, this didn't set too well with many of his subscribers.

But Radcliff often ignored his publisher's advice to write simply. He had a Christian respect for readers, and his editorials were complex and thought-provoking. He signed off his weekly column with the words "More as life unfolds."

And in the stories he chose to run, he often found the humor and delight in small-town incidents. When a fellow came in to place a classified ad:

Found: Pig on golf course.

Owner may have by paying for this ad.

Radcliff followed it up with a story. And that led to others about animals that became a weekly feature for a while.

He also made his mark selling advertising, thus greatly increasing the ad lineage. Much of his success was due to his imaginative approach. Radcliff's ads for John Deere tractors promoted their new executive-style seats, which provided unusual comfort for farmers in the fields. He got the new slim-down center to use the slogan Your Weight Is Over! And he persuaded a plumbing company to promote their services with the motto We Repair What Your Husband Fixed, and a shoe-repair guy to rename his shop The Shoe Hospital and adopt as his motto We Fix Your Sole.

His ideas occasionally backfired. He persuaded the new travel agency to adopt Please Go Away! as their ad slogan. He even printed that phrase on a sign that the owners put on their door. But many a would-be customer took the admonition seriously, and the business went bankrupt.

But mostly his ideas worked. And his success in ad sales meant that the *Courier* didn't have to rely on that staple of small-town weekly newspapers—printing jobs like wedding and farm-sale announcements. In fact, for the past three years, the paper had made a handsome profit, which pleased the owners greatly!

How Radcliff came by his fertile imagination was somewhat of a mystery. The Idea Man had grown up in a very proper, almost Victorian household in a small town nearby. But he had managed to stake out a claim on nuttiness by declaring himself a Professor of Foolology in his freshman year in high school.

In his sophomore year, he had begun an apprenticeship at the local newspaper that eventually included the writing of a weekly gossip column titled "Paper Wads—Thrown by I. Ben Told."

He entered college after high school, but World War II interfered. Before he knew it, he was pounding a typewriter on Amchitka, a cold, remote, and barren island in the Aleutians. There he fought not the enemy, but the tedium and boredom of service life. When a friend committed suicide among all the bleakness, he despaired. And with too much time on his hands, he developed a sort of constant rumbling of the soul.

He read Shakespeare constantly and thought deeply. It led him to ponder manifold things, like why a coffee cup always left a brown ring on a wooden table even when nothing was spilled. And what happens in the cup of coffee when the cream goes in?

It wasn't always clear to him what the cause and effect of things was, and there wasn't much reason in life either! Since the world was nutty and teeming with funny circumstances, Radcliff decided then and there that he'd devote his life to joy and delights. He'd find some genius in just living. He'd take on an irreverent attitude about things and deliciously revel in his sense of the absurd.

Since the WORLD WAS NUTTY AND TEEMING WITH FUNNY CIRCUMSTANCES, RADCLIFF DECIDED THEN AND THERE THAT HE'D DEVOTE HIS LIFE TO JOY AND DELIGHTS.

So he adopted a whimsical spirit and began to regard laughter as the only sane virtue—as James 1:2 in his Bible had it, "count it all joy."

And he took as his personal credo some lines from *In a Garden*, an old 1925 play by Philip Barry that he found in the post library on that desolate Alaskan island: "The heart never grows tired of imagined possibilities; it tires only of possibilities realized."

But it was Radcliff's pursuit of imagined possibilities that brought him into conflict with Senior Warden Harvey Featherstone.

From the very beginning, the two didn't like each other, didn't cotton to the other's way of life, and usually didn't even speak directly to one another. Like an old-fashioned Western, there seemed to be no room for both of them in the little town of Carlson.

Perhaps it was because they were somewhat alike—short and idiosyncratic—even though Featherstone was British. To the core. He was, in fact, more British than anyone should be.

The word *eccentric* seemed to attach itself to him. He had a charming loopiness. Featherstone had settled in Carlson some time before, and through prodigious effort had established a fine career for himself as a ne'er-do-well. His titled family in England sent him money periodically, allowing him a life of undeserved honors and the privilege of keeping himself in style.

After some inexplicable hesitation, he had recently purchased an automobile, but his favorite mode of transportation was the bicycle he rode around town and on church errands while wearing old-fashioned plus-fours. And when he donned trousers, he used big clips at the ankles to keep them from snagging in the pedal mechanism.

The Brit also maintained his English accent. He was prone to pepper his conversation with "Righto" and "I say." He always said "nil" for "zero," addressed every male as "old man," and because he was getting up in years and hard of hearing, much of his conversation consisted of "Eh, what?"

Featherstone lived alone with a housekeeper and her husband in a big house on Elm Street, patterned after the Victorian idea of comfort often espoused by Charles Dickens. That author liked writing about cozy rooms and food and drink and good fellowship. His characters embraced those comforts and so did Featherstone.

After his evening session in his rub-a-dub tub, everything usually seemed clearer. He could then retire to his big chair in the study. It squished when he sat down and displayed a serious dent in its seat when he arose from its depths. From there he would read while a small log fire crackled in the background.

Featherstone had been born (unexpectedly and prematurely) in the Sceptered Isle, at Burnham-on-Sea, where his parents had been on holiday. His mother was a descendant of a fellow who had made a fortune designing and manufacturing women's shoes. He was later knighted by Queen Victoria for his "contributions to British life."

Featherstone had been brought up in an atmosphere of chintz and Chippendale at one of his parents' luxurious flats in London and at his grandparents' twenty-five-room country house in the Cotswolds—"the most English part of England." His mother—cultured, charming, pompous, and indomitable—had little time for the raising of her progeny. Her idea of mothering was to tell the nanny to go see what the children were up to and stop them.

But she did impart to them that wonderful cadence and vocabulary of the English upper classes. Harvey received a comfortable education (taking a first at Cambridge) and learned a smattering of Italian, which was popular at the time. He traveled abroad a bit and then settled down to a gentleman's life at the family's country estate. There he occupied his time with gardening, some walking, and whist. One afternoon a week was spent sipping tea at the vicarage.

His major activity was train spotting—that delightful hobby of certain Englishmen, wherein they identify and then write down the engine number of passing trains. In a country that invented the steam locomotive, it was a legitimate hobby. Harvey and other practitioners hung around train platforms watching the trains go by and jotting down their engine numbers. Then they exchanged sightings by post and in newsletters.

Some folk thought this a bit eccentric, even for Englishmen, and called the lot "puffernutters" or "anoraks," a reference to the Windbreakers they wore to ward off the chill on British train platforms. Harvey and his fellow habitués preferred to be called railway enthusiasts and were undeterred in the pursuit of their passion.

But as he approached his fifties, Featherstone became a bit bored and restive. One day (as he later told the story) he ran into the book *Gentlemen on the Prairie*, by Curtis Harnack, an American author from Iowa. It told the true tale of a gaggle of English aristocrats who attempted to start up a British colony in LeMars, Iowa, in the 1880s. They saw their pioneering efforts as a way of perpetuating the Victorian gentleman's code in America.

These practitioners of serf and turf became entranced by the idea that there was a marked similarity between the uncultivated lands in Iowa and the grounds of certain English estates. They tried to build country houses near LeMars, hoping to become American Lords of the Manor. But when the citizens in the area refused to play their assigned roles as servants, the venture failed, and the noble homesteaders returned home to dear old Blighty.

Featherstone was enchanted by it all! The romance! The adventure! Polo on the prairie! He just had to see the place where it all happened!

So he bought a steamship ticket to the United States and set off to dally in someone else's lost dream. He disembarked a week later in dirty, noisy New York City. There a lady cousin persuaded him to donate some funds to a charity she ran, which supplied trusses to the ruptured poor.

Then he boarded a train for the vast interior of the United States, traveling through the Empire City of Pigs (as his old nineteenth-century guidebook called Cincinnati). He even stopped off in Chicago for the obligatory visit to the Union Stockyards to see cattle being slaughtered.

Jarred by the vigor and brutish vitality of this new land, Featherstone arrived at LeMars in the spring of 1937. He was fascinated by the Iowa landscape with its incredible rectangularity. The orderly neatness of it all boggled the mind! The gridlike checkerboard effect of the land made a curving road—like those back home—a rarity.

There were few traces remaining of the English colony, but he fell in love with the little rolling black hills where life was pretty much something that was happening elsewhere. It all increased his curiosity about the failed venture, so he stayed on in the area, finding a home in nearby Carlson because it boasted an Anglican church. Each year he had intended to return to his native land after he had sorted it all out.

But by now, fifteen years had passed. Slowly he had become used to the Iowa way of pronouncing things like "enaway" and "pert near." Still the natives' habit of responding "you betcha" after he thanked them continued to puzzle him.

A rum leg ("that keeps playing me up a bit") and his age had kept him out of World War II. But Featherstone contributed to the Allied war effort by becoming an Air Raid Warden. Putting to work the keen eye he had acquired during his train-spotting days, he scanned the skies once a week for enemy aircraft from his post atop the Carlson Memorial Library. Later his friends teased him that his presence was responsible for the fact that no Nazi airplanes came even close to Iowa during the entire war!

About the only thing he found wanting in the postwar years was his inability to stop this latest balmy fund-raising idea of his nemesis, Warren E. Radcliff. It annoyed him greatly!

Across town, Shirley Radcliff also frowned in frustration. She knew her husband's new idea about a bear hunt was bound to irritate the Senior Warden and create even more of a rift between the two men. And this would not help her aspirations.

Like Mr. Featherstone, she admired the "agony of the leaves," and she and two of her lady friends often had their own little tea parties on fall afternoons. But she longed to be invited to Featherstone's affairs, which (reports had it) were elaborate soirees with crumpets and delicious scones and jams and clotted cream, as only the true Brits could manage. Moreover, she yearned to be invited to one of his fabulous dinner parties where one would be (she heard) "surrounded by a plethora of words."

She yearned TO BE INVITED TO ONE OF HIS FABULOUS DINNER PARTIES WHERE ONE WOULD BE (SHE HEARD) "SURROUNDED BY A PLETHORA OF WORDS."

Shirley had been happily married for almost ten years now and, as one of her many friends put it, she was one of those who were "admirably disposed to increase and multiply." The couple had three charming children. In almost every way, she was the quintessential 1950s housewife like her fellow Iowan, the TV star Donna Reed.

And her life was pretty normal. Hers was a well-ordered, June Cleaver type of existence. This was good, for Shirley was a primary and necessary force of reason around their home. In the midst of her husband's weird ideas and lifestyle, hers was the voice of caution and stability. As her husband said admiringly, "Everyone needs a person like my Shirley in their lives!"

Her patience had often been tried—particularly early in their marriage. Warren spent a good deal of his time in the smallest room in the house. There he had many an epiphany. The result was that he and his buddy Jeep from his high-school days (who now also lived in Carlson) came up with a lot of juvenile pranks.

Taking advantage of Radcliff's wire recorder, they obtained some sound-effects records and rerecorded the sound of a train, whistle and all. Hooking the wire recorder to a public-address system that they rigged up in Warren's car, they drove to a nearby little town that had never had a railroad track or train depot.

Driving quietly up and down the streets at 2:00 a.m. with their lights off, they broadcast the *chug-chugs* and *toot-toots* to the sleeping citizens. They could scarcely contain their laughter when the upstairs bedroom lights in seven houses went on and the front porch lights at three other residences lit up, before they had to skedaddle. And they reveled in the thought of the tentative, incredulous conversations that must have occurred around town among the puzzled citizens the next morning. "Did you—ah—did you maybe—ah—perhaps possibly hear a train last night?"

On another occasion they got tired of hearing from the salesman at a car dealership about the extraordinary mileage he was getting from his new Chevy. He didn't have a garage and kept his car in his driveway nights, so Radcliff and his buddy filled up the tank on some nights and siphoned out some gas on others. The guy kept going from ecstasy to despair—and drove his mechanic nuts trying to figure it out.

Shirley also had to put up with his enthusiasms of an entrepreneurial nature. Warren would occasionally be inspired by an idea that was going to make them a fortune. She would always listen, and then she would put a stop to it. But she didn't even try to curtail him from putting on a straw hat that was left over from the croquet matches and going to a costume party as The Last Straw. He was that, she sighed, rolling her eyes.

Although Harvey Featherstone pretended to be indifferent to the schemes of lesser men, he had become quite fussed about Radcliff's antics over the years, even though many of them usually had little to do with church activities. The citizens of Carlson talked a lot about them, however, and seemed to get a kick out of them.

But to the Senior Warden, Radcliff's gambols were somewhat corny and obvious. It was as if he was deliberately throwing them—and his Yankee humor and vigor—in Featherstone's determinedly British face.

The Englishman came from "the most English part of England," and Radcliff was a native of "the most American part of America." Two distinct cultures were at war, separated by *more* than a common language.

Not that Featherstone disliked everything about the Colonies. He was an admirer of much of life in the United States. But Radcliff's capers—"Well!" If only he hadn't been away when Radcliff proposed that extraordinary bear project!

Featherstone had been off visiting one of his recently discovered wonders of American life—the trailer court. He loved to drive up and down the mobile parks, looking at the silver Airstreams and Winnebagos in their assigned spaces. He marveled at the picket fences around their trailer hitches and the parakeets in cages hanging from the nearby trees. It gave the places a sort of homey touch. And it was quintessentially American, he thought. Wherever they go, there they are!

In England, the houses were made of stone and most had been

in one place for generations. Here the houses were made of aluminum with wheels on them. The ability to move about the big continent in a house with a license plate was a symbol of the freedom of the New World!

So some things American Featherstone admired. But bears? In the church parking lot?

He determined to try to stop this nonsense. He'd hold one of his famous dinner parties and invite Father Conklin and members of the Vestry. Perhaps he could change their minds.

Featherstone had been forced into giving his much-admired collations in self-defense. After a few months in Iowa, he had despaired of the state's family-style eateries. He was also determined to quash the idea that the only edible meal the British could manage was breakfast. One of his American friends kept teasing him that the Romans had abandoned England in AD 686 because even those hardened warriors could only stand so much of English cooking!

So he had set about learning and instructing his housekeeper in the culinary arts. The two of them pored over recipes and tried out sauces and experimented with different soufflés. They paid special attention to fish dishes since they were a rare delicacy in roast-beef Iowa. And the housekeeper's husband, in white tie and tails, served the meal with as much panache as any former farm boy could muster.

Most of all, Featherstone set a table rich with repartee. He had attended so many dull dinner parties in England, where the jaws of those who had gathered seemed to be set in stone through sheer boredom, that he was determined to make his repasts sparkling.

He usually invited only those whom he felt "could put a sentence or two together," or those businessmen with substantial financial interests. While a few were full of undigested thought, many enlivened the evening with witty banter. Soon Featherstone's "little dinner parties" became the most coveted invitations among the Carlson residents.

So he had little trouble "rounding up the usual suspects," as he put it. Father Conklin and all but one of the Vestry were able to join him at the table.

Although he was certain the company suspected the reason for the dinner and surmised what was coming, the conversation was spirited. The arugula salad with a sherry vinaigrette and the fish filets en papillote brought smiles of appreciation. After the chocolate-almond cake with crème anglaise, the ladies retired to the study and Featherstone came right to the point.

"This bear project is unbecoming," he said. "It should be canceled."

"Oh, Harvey," sighed one of the Vestry patiently. "It's really not so bad."

"But Radcliff is seriously daft!" exclaimed the Senior Warden. "The bloke is barking mad and needs to be locked up!"

One other Vestry member was moved to respond. "I don't know. We need new ideas for fund-raisers, Harvey. Maybe we should bless Radcliff for coming up with all these wild schemes of his. Maybe only some will take, but—"

Featherstone wasn't giving up, however, and he launched into a diatribe that centered on the need for dignity, decorum, and tradition in Anglican matters while most of the Vestry stared at their glasses.

Another member spoke up, however, when the Senior Warden wound down. "I think we ought to look at this compassionately,

Harvey. This bear thing might work out. I voted for it because there's got to come a time when we help a fellow church member from stepping on the rake and hitting himself in the nose." There were nods all around.

Featherstone was not insensitive to the dynamics of the moment and the group's sympathies. He didn't want to seem like the kid banging his spoon on the high chair. So he dropped the matter with a "Why don't we join the ladies?"

But after the guests left, he sought comfort in the study and his familiar chair. There he ruminated about his defeat. This was but one in a series, he thought. Less than a decade before, Britain had scampered out of India, and most recently Egypt had nationalized the Suez Canal, which had been virtually owned by Great Britain since 1882. And now this—this bear thing! The sun was indeed setting on the Empire!

Maybe it was really time for him to return home, to the Land of Hope and Glory. If he could.

But of course he knew (though others didn't) that he couldn't. It was his secret.

So he rose the next morning with a stiff upper lip and a vow to make the best of things.

It was a good thing, for his mettle was about to be tested.

Radcliff was nearly ready to launch the Great Episcopalian Bear Hunt. He had, however, run into a snag.

Parker Wheatly, his sporty fellow Episcopalian, had come down with the measles and couldn't go, and the two other church members who had expressed an interest in the expedition had also dropped out. One guy's mother had just died, and the other's wife wouldn't let him go. "It's all foolishness," she said.

He took his woes to his old buddy Jeep at his sporting-goods store downtown.

"I can't find anybody good to go with me to Canada," he complained.

So Jeep said he'd sign on and let his wife run the store for a while. He also persuaded Radcliff to invite another would-be hunter, "Dingy" Delperdang, to go along. Dingy was a former high-school football hero from the thirties who was frustrated because there were no more games to win—just a sorrowful life to live. He had become such a nonentity that his boss had once called him in and said "Smith, you're fired." So he became self-employed, but got fired again. This had resulted in his determination to spend most of his time down at the pool hall.

Some of the guys there said he was as dumb as concrete. Others maintained that he had forgotten to pay his brain bill and that he couldn't get out of his own way. All agreed that you had to be careful about what you put in Dingy's head because you'd never get it out!

The old football star had never set foot in any church. And so the Great Episcopalian Bear Hunt set off on its mission with only one Anglican member involved. But he—Radcliff—was in charge.

Jeep volunteered his aquamarine-and-cream 1949 station wagon as transportation, and Radcliff arranged a send-off at the church after the coffee hour one early September Sunday. He placed big signs on the sides and back of the vehicle announcing the purpose of the trip to one and all. Father Conklin blessed the car and its occupants, Dingy's wife paraded up and down with a placard that accused him of abandoning his family, and the trio drove off amidst a shower of rice and confetti from Radcliff's children as the public-address speakers on top of the station wagon blared out Patti Paige's version of the top hit of the day, "The Tennessee Waltz!"

Most of the members of the Church of the Heavenly Rest who had turned out for the send-off just looked at one another. Some gaped at the sight. Their "flabber was completely gasted," as one lady put it.

The trio made it to Minneapolis the first night. There Radcliff placed a little sign outside their door at the C'mon Inn that read: We Are Disturbed!

The next day they were on their way northward ho, on dusty two-lane highways dotted occasionally with the famous "rhyming verse by the side of the road"—the Burma Shave signs.

On the second night out, they made it to International Falls, right at the Canadian border, and the next morning they arrived at their jumping-off point—Kenora, Ontario. There they stopped in at the local post of the Royal Canadian Mounted Police and were disappointed that the mountie behind the desk was not dressed like Nelson Eddy. But he directed them to the Ontario Tourism and Information Agency, where they obtained the necessary license to hunt bears. And they found the estate agent who had rented them a hunting/fishing cabin, and who provided them with a key and the directions to it.

With Radcliff navigating, they were off to Pickle Lake. Bouncing over dirt paths chopped out of the wilderness, they went miles without seeing a soul. This was remote, isolated country, with little to boast of but the beauty of the sweet-smelling pines of the north woods. They had to backtrack twice, got lost once again, and stumbled onto a big lodge full of Americans and an Indian guide, who gave them further directions to their cabin in a little clearing by the lake.

The small, two-room log structure was a rather primitive affair with a wood-burning stove that made cooking a challenge. Water had to be carried up from the nearby lake, and there was an outhouse out back. It was, however, somewhat luxurious for the area, having been renovated—like many others in the region—for American sportsmen.

But just as they settled in, the rains came. It poured steadily.

Undeterred, they set out enthusiastically the next morning for their first venture into bear hunting. But after slogging through wet underbrush and slipping down slippery slopes and falling over decaying logs and being almost devoured by mosquitoes as big as birds, they found themselves wet, muddy, and exhausted by midafternoon.

They stopped IN AT THE LOCAL POST OF THE ROYAL CANADIAN MOUNTED POLICE AND WERE DISAPPOINTED THAT THE MOUNTIE BEHIND THE DESK WAS NOT DRESSED LIKE NELSON EDDY.

They had neither smelled, heard, nor sighted any bears. So they retreated to the cabin and a warm fire.

The rain continued the next day, so they clung to the fire and played a bit of pinochle. As they figured it, the bears probably didn't like to go out in the rain either.

They also made their first recording for the folks back home. Setting up the wire recorder by the fire, Radcliff took the mike and described their trip, the cabin, and their first foray into the woods. Jeep chimed in with an anecdote about Dingy and his first attempt at cooking.

To get the recording out to civilization, they walked about a mile to the big lodge and the other Americans. The lodge had a radiophone to the outside world. Radcliffe transmitted the recording back to KHEJ in Carlson, where it was rerecorded for later broadcast on *Aunt Lucy's Morning Show*.

When it continued to rain the next day, the boys remained in their cabin. But to keep to their broadcast schedule, they improvised a fake foray into the woods in search of bears. They got some branches that they brushed against the microphone, blew whooshing sounds across it for the sound of the wind, and faked other noises. Dingy did his best to imitate a bear, but he had never heard one, and his roar sounded more like a cow in heat. They hoped his "Aaurgh" would fool the folks back home.

> *Good morning, folks. This is Warren Radcliff coming to you from the Great Episcopalian Bear Hunt near Pickle Lake, Ontario. We're in our second day of hunting here in the Canadian wilderness (whoosh, whoosh), and let me tell ya, it's exciting! We were up before dawn on this beaut of a day and are now deep in the woods tracking (footsteps) a big black bear. We're on our knees now crawling (sound of brushes) to where we think it is, so I'll have to lower my voice a bit so we won't be heard.*
>
> (Whispering) *I can hear Jeep and Dingy talking (voices muttering) and Jeep is pointing out a cave where he thinks the bear is hiding. Wait, I can hear it! (Aaurgh!) There it goes again! (Aaurgh! Aaurgh!) The bear is out of the cave now and running. We're after it! (Footsteps running and brushes and wood cracking).*

We're chasing it! Jeep is shooting! (gunfire). Oh, we lost it! But we'll keep going (puffing) and trying, 'til we get two of them for the Great Episcopalian Bear Barbecue at the Church of the Heavenly Rest.

This is Warren Radcliff talking (breathing heavily). *We'll report in again tomorrow!*

Sloshing through the rain, the boys took the recording over to the big lodge for transmission back home. The quality of the wire recording was poor at best, the radiophone sounded like those in taxis, and the newly invented Ampex tape recorder back at the radio station left something to be desired in terms of fidelity. So the recording that reached the listeners was filled with static and a lot of noise that covered up much of the hokey homemade sound effects.

But the sound of rain on the tin roof of their cabin came through (when you sensed what it was), and so the boys determined that if they did any more recordings, they'd do them at the larger lodge that had a wooden roof. Besides, they could use some more folks for the sound effects.

So when it was still raining on the fourth day, the other Americans got into the act. They were as rain-bound as the Carlson group, and the little play broke up the monotony. A fellow from Cincinnati made more authentic bear sounds than Dingy, a guy from St. Louis was adept at imitating mosquitoes, and another frustrated hunter cackled (he said) like a wild turkey. Most everybody else thought he sounded like a wounded duck, but amidst the masculine camaraderie, Radcliff allowed him to participate. They were still honest in reporting that they had bagged no bears.

It kept raining, and the boys stayed in the cabin. But later in the week, Radcliff's conscience got the best of him, and he convinced his compatriots to actually go out to hunt. They were skunked again, however, and retreated to do another fake recording. But on their way back to their little cabin to pick up the recording gear, they got a break.

As they trudged down the road, they came across an old beat-up pickup stuck in the mud. Two Indians were attempting to push it out. After the boys had helped them, Radcliff noticed a dead bear under the tarp in the bed of the truck.

"Whaddaya take for that bear?" he asked.

The two Indians looked at one another. "I don't know," said one. "Why don't we get out of this rain and talk about it?"

So they all retired to the boys' cabin and got acquainted. Ronald Bright Trail was the older of the two and did most of the talking. His buddy, Running Chicken, just sort of sat there. Both Indians were Ojibwa.

"That there bear'll come in at about 295 pounds," said Bright Trail, studying the fire.

"More like 250," countered Jeep.

"We'll give you twenty-five dollars," offered Radcliff, looking the Indian straight in the eye.

"Forty," said Bright Trail.

"Thirty-five," countered Radcliff.

"Done," said the Indian, "and we'll clean, dress, and render it for another fifteen."

"Nope," said Radcliff. "Too much."

"Okay," said Bright Trail, "but just be sure to dress it soon. We killed it this morning."

After the Indians left, Radcliff confessed that it wasn't the money that prevented him from agreeing to have the Indians butcher the animal. They needed a big intact bear on the front of the station wagon when they drove into Carlson to convince the residents of their prowess and to promote the barbecue.

The rain let up a bit to a fine drizzle on their last day for hunting, and they tried again with no luck. But they went back to the big lodge and reported a kill in their transmission back to Carlson, for by now they had become sort of persuaded that they—not the Indians—had brought down the bear that was now tied to the hood of Jeep's station wagon. And Radcliff had a plan to end their expedition on an even brighter note.

Bright Trail had told him of a meat-locker store in Kenora that often had bear meat for sale. So they packed up and, on their way through the town to drop off the key to the cabin, they bought some bear meat at Finnigan's Locker. They purchased the equivalent of a 300-pounder in small bruin chops, suitable for barbecuing and, flushed with success, set out for home.

On their way down to the lower forty-eight, they stopped at a town and phoned a made-up story of their last "kill" back to the radio station.

By sheer luck, Radcliff reported, *Dingy bagged a three-hundred-pounder with one shot on our way out of Pickle Lake.* They themselves had butchered it on the spot, he said. *The bear chops are ready!*

To time their arrival at the church during the Sunday morning coffee hour, the boys stayed at a motel just over the state line in Minnesota for a night. Radcliff put another little sign on the doorknob that read, Do Not Disturb Further.

The boys turned on the PA system in some of the little towns they passed through later on and promoted the Great

Episcopalian Bear Barbecue, which they promised would "set the world's bellies on fire." And then they blew into Carlson on a quiet Sabbath morn with the loudspeakers blaring the newly popular song "On Top of Old Smokey."

The good members of the Church of the Heavenly Rest were drawn outside by the music, to be confronted by the old station wagon, almost invisible under the dried mud, with a black bear stretched over the hood. Three dirty, unwashed, and bearded occupants emerged from its interior. Harvey Featherstone walked off in a huff, but the boys were greeted warmly by the congregation. The radio reports had done their work, and the church members were getting excited! Father Conklin said a brief prayer of thanksgiving and led everyone in three "Hip Hip Hoorays!"

The next morning the boys dropped off the bear at a local meat shop for skinning and butchering and put the bear chops in its refrigeration locker. Jeep and Radcliff went back to work, but Radcliff spent much of the next week finalizing plans for the barbecue and promoting the event on the radio station.

And on a bright Saturday afternoon, many of the citizens of Carlson and the surrounding area gathered in the parking lot of the Church of the Heavenly Rest for the Great Episcopalian Bear Barbecue. They were greeted by some unusual music.

Radcliff had engaged a popular polka band out of Sioux City—the Six Fat Dutchmen—to play on a flatbed truck during the feast. It was a wise choice. While the church members barbecued and served the food, the customers ate bear, and enjoyed the polkas.

And before the day was over, the members of the church's barbecue team had served up 300 pounds of coleslaw, 1,900 bags of potato chips, 800 soft drinks, 100 gallons of coffee—and 500 pounds of bear meat. The bear meat had enough fat to put a few cardiologists' kids through college, but oh—did it ever taste good!

The event was a smashing success! They took in enough money to pay for more than half of a new roof, the church got some much-needed publicity, and the people of Carlson got to know more about the Episcopalians and found out that they weren't stuck up at all.

Everyone went home happy—everyone except Harvey Featherstone. He had refused to attend the event.

The glow of success lasted about four hours. Along about eight o'clock that night, some of the folk who had attended the affair began to phone their doctors. A few went to the emergency room of the local hospital. All complained of stomach pains, vomiting, and diarrhea. The physicians treated them and exchanged notes and finally concluded that nearly half the people who had attended the bear barbecue that day had food poisoning!

The physicians TREATED THEM AND . . . FINALLY CONCLUDED THAT NEARLY HALF THE PEOPLE WHO HAD ATTENDED THE BEAR BARBECUE THAT DAY HAD FOOD POISONING!

Oh, it wasn't any deadly form of bacteria. This was a minor case of gastrointestinal difficulty that created a lot of discomfort but was not serious. The condition was temporary and would pass in a day or so with little intervention by the physicians.

But when he heard about it the next day, Radcliff was devastated. Comforted by Shirley, he holed up in his house, as did Jeep.

But down at the pool hall, the fellows questioned Dingy and eventually wormed the truth out of him. He explained about the constant rain and told them about the fake radio broadcasts and the purchase of the meat from Finnigan's Locker and how they bought a bear from the Indians.

It must have been that one that had caused the poisoning, he said. It had been dead for too long when they got it back to Carlson for butchering.

When Featherstone heard the news, he was ecstatic. *Now I've got him*, he thought. *Radcliff's done it this time!* And in a fit of happy ferocity, he proceeded to set up an "enquiry into the barbecue matter" by the Vestry. All knew he would push for a censure of Radcliff and, at the least, a ban on any more of his ideas at the church, "now and in perpetuity."

When Jeep heard about the Senior Warden's plans, he was furious. This was unfair! Sure, they had cheated a little bit on the radio reporting of the expedition, and he was sorry that some folk got a little sick. But the proposed punishment did not fit the crime. The church had raised a significant amount of money, and people had enjoyed themselves. Besides, what would his old friend Warren do if he didn't have an outlet for his wonderful imagination?

So Jeep set out to try to undermine Featherstone's plan. He contacted an old navy buddy of his in London who had stayed in the service after World War II. The friend was in naval intelligence (although Jeep thought that nomenclature was the ultimate in oxymoronic phrases), and he pleaded with his old friend to launch a quiet investigation into the background of one Harvey Featherstone. Was there anything he could use?

And they struck pay dirt. While Featherstone's tale about coming to America after being inspired by a book about English colonists in Iowa was true enough, it wasn't quite the whole story.

He had indeed emigrated from the Cotswolds, where the

tranquil villagers led lives that usually—and wisely—tolerated the calm relationship between the conventional and the eccentric, and among the landed gentry and the underclasses.

But the naval officer unearthed the fact that Featherstone had backed over the foot of a footman on the family estate with his Morgan motorcar on three separate occasions! The servants had become restive. And before Featherstone could be questioned about the third incident by the local constabulary, he had fled to America.

"He was," wrote the authorities, "quite seriously out of sorts." And their solution was to let the Colonists deal with him in the future. They had simply listed him in the record books as "gone missing."

When Jeep quietly presented these facts to Featherstone, the Brit could only mutter, "Bit of a sticky wicket, wot?" But knowing that the task of any sensible gentleman was to get out of any problematic situation and into comfort at any cost, he compromised. He said he simply couldn't afford to have the motorcar incidents known by his community of friends in the New World here in Carlson, Iowa.

So in exchange for Jeep's silence about the motorcar matter, the Senior Warden promised to stop the enquiry into the bear barbecue and not to interfere with any of Radcliff's further presentations of fund-raising ideas to the Vestry. Moreover, he would put things right by inviting Radcliff and his wife over for a peacemaking dinner.

But Featherstone was full of guile and Machiavellian plots, and he had one more angle to play. So he made some phone calls and sat back and waited for the "make-up dinner."

There were only four guests that evening—Father Conklin and his wife, and Radcliff and his Shirley, who was ecstatic at the invitation.

It was a particularly salubrious affair. The banter was stimulating, and Radcliff's thoughts so engaging that Featherstone actually began to take a liking to—and appreciation of—the Idea Man. He discovered their mutual admiration for the "zounds" and "forsooths" of Shakespeare, and became in awe of his old nemesis's fertile and imaginative mind. Underneath Radcliff's daffiness lay some basic human truths.

The Brit was further moved by the sudden realization that in everyone's life there are a chosen few—like Radcliff—who are destined to see and take things farther than the rest of us. They are the observers. They are the visionaries. They are the clowns. And they should be cherished, for they are engaged in fashioning the wondrous ideas that celebrate life!

The cordiality around the table was infectious, so much so that during the meal, the priest was moved to a toast. "Sometimes you eat the bear, sometimes the bear eats you, and sometimes you and the bear just sit together in the night. Well done!"

After the sumptuous meal and Featherstone's presentation of a Brown Betty Teapot to a happy Shirley, Father Conklin led the wives to the study, leaving Radcliff and his host alone.

The Senior Warden cleared his throat. "How would you like the job of executive secretary of the Carlson Chamber of Commerce? It would give you a wonderful outlet for your—ah—ideas. You can use just about any scheme to promote the town and bring shoppers downtown. Bill Jennings will be leaving, and I could arrange it for you to be his replacement."

Radcliff stammered, "Well—ah—I don't know—how much does it pay?"

"Twice your present salary, and there are excellent health and retirement plans."

"Well—uh—I don't know. You say I'd have free rein for my ideas?"

"Yes—but there is one condition," said the Senior Warden. "You'll have to stop presenting those cockamamie fund-raising proposals to the Vestry. Save your imaginative ideas for your new and bigger job in civilian life. You'll have more luck and fun with them there. What say you?"

Radcliff shifted in his seat, then grinned and nodded. It would certainly be a new challenge, as well as a chance to revel in his own sense of the absurd on a much bigger canvas—the whole town and surrounding shopping area! What an opportunity!

So the two sealed the bargain and then joined the others in the study. There Featherstone announced the deal, and Radcliff regaled them all with some of the ideas he already had for his new job—ideas that he had been mulling over in his mind, but that were not quite right for Episcopal fund-raisers.

Perhaps they could stage the Giant Tomato Fight at First and Main some Saturday night using ripe tomatoes! In August everyone had more than they could give away. So they'd collect them and truck in a couple more tons of the fruit from other towns. People could fling the red objects at one another, resulting in a gooey, sticky, slushy mess!

"Think of the aggressions that would be released! One could fire away at an old enemy! Teenagers could pelt their parents!" he said enthusiastically.

And as his tongue continued to almost outrace his thoughts, he turned to musical events. Maybe they could book that tuba choir from Cuba, or benefit from his wartime service in the Aleutians by bringing down the Eskimo Marching Band for a concert.

If all that was too expensive, perhaps they could establish the Gallery of Bad Arts and Crafts. Taking advantage of the awful dreadfulness of many of the local arts and crafts, like those created by the Episcopalian ladies, they could set up exhibits in the municipal building. People would be attracted to the breathtaking badness of it all, and the submissions would continue to come in because it would be a win-win situation. If a contributor's work was accepted, she could say that she had something that was shown in a gallery. If her submission was rejected, she could boast that a gallery had determined that it was "not bad."

Maybe they could even launch the National Anvil Flight Invitational out at the ballpark. Guys would put an anvil on top of gunpowder and set it off—and *blam!*—the thing would soar into the sky. The contestants would be judged by how high and how far the anvil flew and the manner of its landing. "Folks would come out to see that, wouldn't they—and then they'd shop downtown!" enthused the Idea Man.

And as his wife pulled him out the door and drove them off, Featherstone heard one last thought from his new friend, shouted as he leaned out of the open car window. It was a stage direction from Shakespeare's *A Winter's Tale.*

"Exit, pursued by bear!" hollered the gleeful Radcliff. And he was gone—into the night and into his bright and active future!

Everybody said the Church of the Heavenly Rest was never quite the same after that night. Some folks said that was a pity.

Story 6

Meanwhile,
Back at the
Manse

AT THE MANSE

"I kid you not," she said.

They all leaned forward for more.

"They found him dancin' cheek-to-cheek with the cold cement. He said he drank so much that he passed out 'cause Olive told him that she couldn't be his 'sweet thang' anymore, after she caught him in the ladies' room with Gloria Jenkins during the firemen's benefit dance. The Western Playboys were playin' 'I Been Flushed from the Bathroom of Your Heart' at the time," cackled Myrtle.

There was a collective gasp from the ladies of the Ruth Circle. This one was better than the usual gossip from Myrtle. She was on a roll today!

They were in their knitting-chatting mode after the monthly inspirational and business meeting, and as they sipped their coffee and the needles flew, they relished the opportunity to "share their thoughts." That's how Pauline Washburn characterized their tattle, anyway.

Pauline was like that. She always managed to glorify the mundane. Part of it was the result of her addiction to simple poetry and romance novels. She was prone to quote Edgar Guest without even giving a person some warning. And she loved the new paperback books and popular songs featuring glamorous ladies who found love in "faraway places with strange-sounding names," while wearing some "red silk stockings and the green perfume."

She was addicted to that too. The olfactory senses, that is. Pauline could spend an hour at Needrow's Drug Store, sampling heady mixtures of cloying aromas. She was currently in the thrall of a fragrance called Viva Vita, a mixture of hyacinths, violets, and forget-me-nots, with just a hint of rose.

"You have to wear it at various times of the day to determine how it smells during your different moods," she explained to the girls, as she batted the eyelashes that her enemies said could wash windows. "Sometimes it brings out all my unpredictability, and at other times, I grow madly in love with its fabulous, full-bodied, feminine scent. Either way," she said pretentiously, "it makes a serene and serendipitous statement!"

The ladies' eyes rolled 'round with that one. Pauline could make one do that. She used such language and the perfume, some said, to counter her husband's occupation. For "Doc" Washburn was the area's veterinarian who specialized in large ranch animals and spent much of his time "doing the unspeakable to their unmentionables," according to Pauline.

Across the room, Mickie Hicky was fascinated by the news of the new perfume and vowed right there and then to get some the next time she was down at the drugstore. "I'll bet it'll go goo-ood with ma neuw dress!" she enthused in her South Dakota twang, which often dropped g's from words that didn't even have them. But then Mickie was like that.

She was a red-haired, freckled young lady who was about three bricks shy of a load, according to some of the guys down at the pool hall. Someone once asked her if she had ever read Shakespeare and she said, "No, who wrote it?"

And before Myrtle corrected her, Mickie had thought that the name of Noah's wife was Joan of Ark. It made all sorts of sense, she said, indignantly.

She also struggled to understand the Scripture lessons. The language was obscure, and the references to the various biblical tribes confusing. At one meeting she had broken up the little group by asking what Phyllis the Philistines were named after.

Mickie also had a bashful bladder, struggled with her weight, and the sides of her were remarkably cantilevered. She had spent most of her life pushing reluctant flesh into places it didn't want to go. The boys down at the pool hall described her as a middleweight.

Her taste in clothing was also suspect. Some of the ladies could only offer her their "sincere regrets," when they saw one of her new outfits.

But the Ruth Circle of the First Presbyterian Church of Grand Meadow, South Dakota, which was gathered there, was awfully fond of her. Many of them also fought "the battle of the bulge," and Mickie wasn't truly a fruitcake and certainly not a bimbo. She was more of a chickie—a bit naive—wide-eyed and open-mouthed. And she always seemed to be genuinely surprised and happy about something.

Sometimes it was her kids and sometimes her music playing.

She had taken up the xylophone shortly after her marriage to a brawny guy by the name of Bill. One of the requirements for playing the instrument was to have a big husband and a truck to transport the thing. Bill worked as a general handyman for the town and owned his own Chevy pickup, so he fit the bill nicely.

And besides, he thought the name she acquired when she married him—Mickie Hicky—was, quite simply, a lovely poem. Mickie was only up to one mallet in each hand on the instrument now, but she was improving. So much so that she had wrangled an invitation to play at the Better Grand Meadow Club meeting the next week. As she told the president, "Ah have really an' trulee suffered for ma music, an' naow it's your turn!" He managed to keep a straight face.

AROUND TOWN

The Better Grand Meadow Club attempted to foster business in the little burg of fewer than 900 souls. It was (folks said) "an island in a sea of land." The town was located "west of the river" (as South Dakotans have it), which meant that it was a part of the endless plains and ranch country west of the Missouri River ("the shoreline of the prairie," according to some wags). But it was east of Rapid (City, that is).

In the late 1950s, it was a community usually undimmed by human tears. There was little crime or tragedy in a place where rugged and tanned cowpokes in worn Levi's believed that hard work never killed anybody and that success could be achieved by anyone if they just put their hands to it. They labored resolutely alongside one another on the harsh, wind-swept prairie "where the skies were not cloudy all day" and men were men and women weren't.

It was a place where the sheer vastness of the landscape

threatened to overwhelm the residents, and the wind blew constantly. It was often faster than a guy's pickup. Some old boys down at the pool hall maintained that one day in 1949 the wind had stopped blowing, and everybody fell over.

The town's role in life was to support the sale of cowboy hats and the cattle ranching in the area, where the difference between prosperity and ruin was only about seven cents a pound. The little oasis of civilization sustained the hard life of calving and branding and the laconic speech and horse sense of rough string-riders with aching shoulders who could spit with authority. Most could light a wooden match with a fingernail.

The wranglers were hard on horses and women, in an immense land where "it's your misfortune and none of my own" was the golden rule. The big sky could always be seen by looking straight ahead in a pasture so vast that one could wear out a pretty good horse just gettin' across it.

At least that was what a tenderfoot bragged one day at the bar down at the pool hall. His boast about his new spread was greeted with a polite silence, broken only by an old-timer two stools down, who straightened up at the mention of the horse. "Yep," he said, "I had a poorly one like that back in '34."

When they weren't selling goods or educating children, the folks in Grand Meadow sat outside on their front porches in lawn chairs at summer sundowns to watch a car drive by on the dusty streets every fifteen minutes or so. The town was a place of side doors and back doors, where no one ever knocked at the front door. Too formal.

If one did drop in with some extra cucumbers from her garden, she didn't interrupt the housewife at her kitchen chores. Their work was important—the most vital aspect of life in the region.

Meanwhile, *Back at the* Manse

For their menfolk relied on mouth-watering food to fuel their bodies and provide the energy for the hard work they endured in wresting a living from the land. They had gargantuan appetites and two-fisted eating habits and were proud of their ability to shovel it in. And they were also silently proud of their wives' skills in providing them with tasty vittles. A good cook was indispensable—as important to a man as a good rope—and good cookin' took time and care.

So, while the lady of the house continued to chop or peel or mix, the visitor sat by, sipping some coffee and chattering about everything and nothing. Visiting and gabbing were warm rituals.

Unless, of course, she was a member of one of the town's churches and their ladies' groups. They had their own talky habits.

The fair sex who were members of a particular church met periodically on a weekday afternoon for a light worship session, a moral or spiritual lesson by one of the members, some planning for (or work on) some charity projects, and (not incidentally) some gossip.

The cacophony of soprano voices was wondrously comforting for them all. Depending on the time of their meetings, the groups usually enjoyed a "delicious lunch" or "repast," as it was always called in the resulting story in the next issue of the weekly *Grand Meadow Bugle*.

St. Paul's Lutheran, with its Scandinavians, had the largest number of persons of the female persuasion involved in such activities. The Good News Gospel Church also had its women's group, and the Presbyterians brought up the rear with a relatively new gaggle of fourteen ladies.

All of the groups were adept at launching potluck dinners, although none featured food as tasty as the fare reportedly served at the Catholic Church over in Ida Grove. The Protestants called that place (somewhat enviously) the Church of the Immaculate Kitchen. But the Presbyterians with their noted penchant for good eating had, by common consensus, the best cooks, in Grand Meadow, that is.

> *In addition to* THE LITTLE BIT OF RELIGIOSITY, THE MONTHLY MEETINGS THAT BROUGHT THEM TOGETHER HAD BECOME PART CULTURAL EXCHANGE, PART GABFEST, PART CONFESSIONAL.

The local version of the United Presbyterian Women (UPW) had been resurrected two years earlier and was divided into two small groups, organized according to when it was convenient for the members to meet. Ruth Circle, led by The Minister's Wife, met on the second Thursday of every month at 1:30 p.m. at her home—the Manse. There were five of them in the aggregation.

The ladies always drove to the meetings separately. There was no sharing of rides. It was like they didn't trust one another's driving skills.

But they trusted one another in every other way—implicitly. After all, they were all of an age where—to their dismay—they were beginning to look and act like their mothers. And as one of them remarked without irony, "At least we aren't men!"

In addition to the little bit of religiosity, the monthly meetings that brought them together had become part cultural exchange, part gabfest, and part confessional. They could share beauty tips, some occasionally inward feelings, and some gripes about the menfolk.

In a time and place that was dominated by cowboy boots and

bowlegged masculinity, it was a sanctuary where the women could nod knowingly to one another. In their female camaraderie, they found a sense of harmony that each had wished for but never quite known.

MEANWHILE, BACK AT THE MANSE

So it was with increasing interest that the ladies listened to Myrtle's next tale about the goin's-on around town. She asked them if they had noticed the little one-inch ad placed in the *Bugle* that day. She pulled out the newspaper and read it:

FOUND

Money. Owner may claim by properly identifying.
See Ann or Bob at Needrow's Drug.

"Who could have lost it?" she asked. Everyone turned for an answer to superior Pauline, who shook her head.

"How much was it?" wondered Mickie. "It certainly had ta be enuf ta make it worthwhile placin' tha ad." And she speculated that it must be less than $25. "More'n that an' Ann an' Bob woulda prob'ly phoned tha town marshal."

"Well, it certainly wasn't a little amount like $5, because that small of a pecuniary asset would have barely paid for the ad," sniffed Pauline in her inflated way. And they all agreed that the sum was not enough to matter, but just enough to care.

"It prob'ly weren't in no billfold or a purse, or tha ad woulda said that," volunteered Mickie. "It was prob'ly bills—not small change—bills all wadded up like. I wonder who found it," she mused.

Whoever it was (they all agreed solemnly) was an honest person. And what could Ann or Bob do once it was found and turned in to them? Whoever lost it evidently didn't miss it immediately. Since it wasn't a criminally large amount or a piddlin' small sum, what does a person do? "You can't go around inquiring of every future customer who comes in the door if they have misplaced some money," sniffed Pauline.

"So you hold right on to it for a coupla days an' if noboody claims it, ya put an ad in tha *Bugle*," volunteered Mickie.

"But how do you write an ad for lost money?" asked The Minister's Wife.

"Carefully," said Myrtle.

And everybody laughed.

"The ad didn't say that the owner could have the money by paying for the ad, like they usually do," Myrtle continued. "It just said that the owner could have it by 'properly identifying it.'"

"But how does one go about identifying money?" asked The Minister's Wife. "Outside of the fact that it's green, who remembers the exact kind of money they have on them? Do you have four five-dollar bills or four one-dollar bills or what?"

"Anyhoo," said Mickie righteously, "tha most important thang heah is ta find out whomsoever lost it."

And that led to further speculation about the identity of the loser.

Could it have been old Harry Hopkins copping a look at *True Confessions* at the magazine rack? Or some kid who was picking out a Mother's Day card with his savings? Or perhaps someone who came in for a Coke?

The fifth member of the group finally joined in the discussion. "Maybe it was old Widow Thompson who might have dropped some bills on the floor while she fumbled with her purse at the prescription counter," said Connie.

She had been silent up to now, attending to her knitting and her coffee. She was prone to do that, for she prided herself on being a woman of few words.

Connie stood more than six feet tall, and her big frame seemed to fill a room. She had eyes that were too close together, and the front of the top of her was oversupplied.

Her daddy had been "rich and her ma good-looking," but she had inherited the former quality rather than the latter. In spite of her size and looks, her eyes were tiny in the fullness of her face and they burned brightly when she was running things. When she said, "Do it!" one did it!

All except her husband, that is. He was not intimidated by her or her ways. George was a big guy himself who had been quite an athlete in high school and joined the army right afterward. Then he made an attempt at higher education.

They had married after he dropped out of college, in spite of the rumors that had surrounded Connie's college life. One of her sorority sisters down at USD (University of South Dakota) said that the guys in Connie's life were so numerous that a few years after graduation they had considered holding a reunion!

Connie's marriage to George was welcomed by her family, and he had used her inheritance to found the Brownfield Insurance Company in town. George was also now the Mayor of Grand Meadow, but it was only a part-time position. And although Connie had strong opinions about everything, she and George had come to an accommodating understanding. Neither told the other what to do or how much to say.

AROUND TOWN

For George *was* a talker. It fit his profession as an insurance salesman. People who kept waiting for him to run down and out of things to say finally bought from him in desperation.

He had, said some, "the ability to sing the birds out of the trees." The Good News Gospel Church people allowed as how he had probably received "the gift of tongues."

That's sort of how he got to be elected Mayor. Because he seldom stopped talking, he had come out on most sides of most issues over the years, and that endeared him to many voters. Others said they voted for him just to shut him up.

And to his and others' surprise, he was not bad at the job. He was now in his third term, and his town position had really helped his insurance business. Sometimes you couldn't tell where his official pronouncements left off and his sales pitch began.

His duties as Mayor were usually quite routine. He had to mediate the battles between two elderly neighbors, one of whom was always late in shoveling his sidewalk after a snowstorm and the other who, in retaliation, never got around to mowing his lawn before it got to be six inches in height.

And he had to coordinate things with the Better Grand Meadow Club, which sought to encourage business "downtown," as the merchants called it. The residents called the area "uptown," but either way they were describing the two blocks of what the Mayor liked to call the Business District.

He also had some real problems. The Grand Meadow Rescue Unit needed a new van, and they didn't have it in the budget. Old Man Evans's hogs were celebratin' Valentine's Day early and frightening the elementary-school kids who had to pass his pigpen every day. And as Mayor, he had been asked to throw out the first fish of the season at nearby Lake Lemon. He couldn't imagine how he was going to do that!

Then there was this business of The Lost Money. So he stopped into Needrow's to ask about it.

The drugstore was one of six establishments that weren't boarded up in the dying Business District. It was a hangout for the high-school kids, who went there to see and be seen after school hours. The boys usually sat at the counter, while the girls plunked down in the two little booths near the soda fountain, sipping Cokes, giggling, and eying the guys in their tight jeans. The setting set all their adolescent hearts atwitter and the girls' hearts, in particular, to going *boom boom*.

And it was heaven for the jocks to strut into the place after a game, with hair still wet from the shower and smiles of victory on their faces. Those smiles were seldom seen, however, for the Grand Meadow Larks had a history of being on the wrong end of the score.

Some said it was their nickname. How could they see themselves as killers on the football field or winners on the basketball court with the image of a tweeting little bird in their minds? And the cheer

> *Fight, Larks, Fight.*
> *Tear 'em up,*
> *Bust 'em up,*
> *Fight, Larks, Fight!*

seemed—well—silly.

Back in the '40s, there *had* been a movement to change the nickname and, while they were at it, the school colors of red and white. Wartime inferior fabric had caused the new uniforms for both the football and basketball teams to fade, and after repeated washings, the red had become a sort of pinkish color.

This was the last straw for some of the former jocks around town, who pleaded with the principal to get a new nickname and colors for the high-school athletic teams. The administrator put it to a student vote, sure that it would pass, but he hadn't counted on many of the wives in the area who were also alumnae of the school. Some of them were former cheerleaders, and they worshiped the nickname and the colors. They persuaded the girls to vote no, and since the girls outnumbered the boys in high school at the time, the idea failed.

In a town THAT WAS PRETTY TOLERANT OF THINGS, WHERE PEOPLE SELDOM CARED ABOUT WHAT ONE DID AS LONG AS THEY KNEW ABOUT IT, MYRTLE PROVIDED A LOT OF THAT KNOWLEDGE.

To take the sting out of the defeat, the principal did order new uniforms. But they didn't help much.

In their first football game in the new duds, the Larks got beat 67 to 6. Their only touchdown came just before the half when a whistle blew and the other team left the field. According to Bob Needrow (who was a decent halfback himself in his school days), it still took the Larks two plays to score!

And Bob was ready to answer the query from the Mayor about The Lost Money. "Nope," he said, "nobody's claimed it yet."

MEANWHILE, BACK AT THE MANSE

After offering her theory to the group about who had lost the money, the Mayor's wife returned to her silence. Connie always prided herself on knowing when to shut up.

Which was more than one could say about Myrtle. She was as loquacious as Connie was brusque and had a tendency to employ her mouth before she engaged her brain.

She could—and did—rattle on about everything, for she had no hair growing on her tongue, as the Spanish would say. Even in the heat of summer, she brought to the meetings the caustic tongue of winter. Myrtle didn't seem to like people very much.

Some said that if you called her on the telephone, you sometimes got an ear infection.

It appeared to them that Myrtle was always out of sorts. If that wasn't enough, she had recently given up smoking. Again.

Her father had been a Presbyterian missionary to the Pine Ridge Indian Reservation a little ways to the south, and had died of that occupation. Perhaps she was mad at that.

Maybe she had just been born with a contrary disposition. One of her old Sunday school teachers remembered that when Myrtle was growing up, even her imaginary playmates ran away from her. Perhaps she was mad at that.

She had been engaged at the beginning of World War II and had said a tearful good-bye down at the railroad station to a home-town soldier who never came back. He wasn't killed or anything like that—he just never came back. Perhaps she was mad at that.

Myrtle was a maiden lady of German extraction who loved the concept of schadenfreude—that wonderful Teutonic delight that one takes at the misfortunes of others. When the rude or foolish got their comeuppance, it brought a small smile to her thin lips.

Like when a car driven by a teenager passed her going 65 mph in a 35-mph zone, and later down the road she saw that he had been picked up by the town marshal. Last year she had particularly enjoyed running into another old flame who had dumped her for a young blonde, who later became (she heard) a nun.

She reveled in those moments and in her ability to prattle on, and the members of Ruth Circle reveled in her revelations. For she said things the others only wondered about. In a town that was pretty tolerant of things, where people seldom cared about what one did as long as they knew about it, Myrtle provided a lot of that knowledge.

They got to know who had been caught doing married things before the marriage, and who was having money trouble, and whose kid was having academic problems at Grand Meadow High. Where did she get such information? they asked themselves one day when she was out of the room. How did she know so much about so many?

Pauline was of the opinion that Myrtle was just naturally curious and had no shame. "She'll ask anybody anything," she whispered reprovingly in her la-de-da manner.

Connie's theory was that Myrtle paid people to tell her things. "Not much, mind you, but a dollar here and a dollar there," she said.

The Minister's Wife had the most charitable explanation, for her husband's occupation, combined with her own inclinations to be kind, had become something of a moral imperative. "Myrtle's got big ears," she said. (She did.) "And people just naturally turn to such folk with their gossip."

Everyone agreed that Myrtle's chatter was almost always accurate. She knew who was doing what to whom and who had gone where for what reason. The lady was a veritable water fountain of information, with a dry sense of humor and an ability to find the absurdities in life.

When Connie lapsed into silence about The Lost Money during the coffee hour, gossipy Myrtle knew it was time to move on. "Did you hear that Mrs. Peckensnider is pregnant again? It's the fourth time in six years!" she said. That news drew clucks all around and reminded Pauline that she had to get their dog spayed. She'd get her Doc to do it next week.

And that led her to silently ponder the doglike behavior of men. It was becoming a favorite topic of the group—men's behavior, that is. They returned to it often. It had all started with

Mickie, who said that her husband should get their phone installed down at the pool hall 'cause he all but lived there anyway. And then somebody griped about the awful table manners and the big appetites of the men she helped feed at roundup time.

Then Pauline mentioned that she had just seen a Sandra Dee movie where a mother had advised her daughter to handle guys like dogs. "Why can't we apply the training we give dogs to men?" she offered, looking toward Myrtle for approval. "I'm serious."

"Sure," chuckled Mickie. "An' since both critters like ta mark thar territory with thar smell or some favorite thang, let 'im put his dirty underweah in tha same place on the floah each time he

takes 'em off. An' don't pick 'em up an wash 'em. When tha pile gets ta be high enuf, he'll put 'em in the hamper an thank it was his idee an' his speshul place!" Everybody laughed.

Connie, as usual, had the last word. "And make sure to be firm, but not too firm, on the leash," she said with a grin. "Anything that has been forced into captivity will want to get out and run around with the pack. If a guy goes off nights to be with the boys, don't chase after him. He'll just do it more often to have fun running away. Pretend you're having a ball without him, and he'll come back to you with his tail wagging, wanting to play." There were snickers all around.

The Minister's Wife sensed the analogies might be getting out of hand and suggested an end to the meeting. "The kids will be coming home from school soon," she said. And as they gathered up their things and she saw the group out the door, she sighed a bit.

Another one down, The Minister's Wife thought.

She picked up the living room and waited for her kids, who were bound to be in some serious need of milk and cookies. They were the Presbyterian-issued, towheads-with-blue-eyes, who were seven and nine years old and (to put it kindly) "a challenge."

They weren't really bad—just boys. When they were being that, however, she often thought about the old saying that children are a blessing that you may not have asked for, but if you complain, God will give you something worse.

The oldest was particularly mischievous. He always jumped on the bell hose two or three times at the Skelly gas station uptown every time he passed it, thereby making "dings" back in the garage and annoying the thunder out of old Cletus

Hornbacker, the owner. Mr. Hornbacker was usually under the hood of somebody's car and had to stop whatever he was doing to look up to see if he had a new customer.

And the oldest was forever telling the little girls in the neighborhood that if they swallowed their gum, it would stick on the inside of them, and they would get a terrible stomachache and die. He swore it, by using two fingers to cross his chest. And since he was a preacher's kid, they believed him.

The Minister's Wife did manage to get the boys scrubbed up with clean necks and ears every Sunday and dress them up so they looked respectable. Most of the congregation, though, thought the rapscallions were cute, and dismissed their antics because they were PKs and therefore had enough of a hard row to hoe in life anyhow.

But The Minister's Wife worried about them. There wasn't much for them to do in the little town, particularly on the warm, empty days of summer when the cries of children playing "Ole Ole Olsen, All in Free!" drifted on the evening air. How could she keep them out of mischief?

Lately she had been thinking that maybe the town should build a new playground. The one in the park had been put up in the '30s and consisted of a rusty swing set and a beat-up old slide. A little boy had died there last month. The 25-year-old equipment wasn't to blame though. He had just been running and fell on his head. Still . . .

The playground at the school wasn't much better, and it was difficult to get any kids to go there when school wasn't in session. It was too much of a reminder of how short summer was. Maybe she'd make some calls and broach the idea of a new playground with her husband at suppertime.

AROUND TOWN

The Minister was on his rounds. This was his afternoon for visitations to the ailing and ancient members of his congregation. He had finished his little chat with Widow Thompson, who was so old (according to Widow Humphrey) that she was around for the Virgin Mary's baby shower. And he had just completed his visit to Widow Humphrey, who (Widow Thompson said) was so old that she had ridden a horse to get on Noah's ark.

The Minister had recently restored an old custom. He had the sexton toll the years of a person's life on the church bell at the funeral. He had the good sense to curtail the tolling when any old woman died, because the rope and the ancient bell wouldn't stand it. But he wondered which one of the quarreling, cantankerous old ladies would die first, and what the other one would have to say about it.

As he started to get into his car to drive out to Lyle Grover's ranch to visit Lyle's brother, who was suffering from lumbago, he paused to gaze out past Widow Humphrey's tidy front lawn. She lived on the edge of town, and as he looked past her garage, he could see the stultifying uniformity of the vast western prairie, where the horizon went on forever. The countryside was so broad you could see the wind patterns playing across the grassy pastures.

It was a still and quiet land where "seldom was heard a discouraging word." The flat, unrelenting spaces made him want to run back to the forested Adirondacks of his childhood and revel in the towering pines.

The Minister came from a long line of Calvinist preachers who were forced to leave Scotland because (as the family joke had it) "they wanted to sing the psalms through their noses." So he had a "good clerical name," and he had charged into the ministry like he was auditioning for the role of Moses.

But he soon found out that much of the job was to baptize, marry, and preside over funerals or, as his more experienced ministerial colleagues put it, "hatch, attach, and dispatch." It had begun to wear on him.

He HAD experienced some success in his parish. He started a mimeographed newsletter he titled the Lamplighter. Now as new members began to slightly outnumber the ones who died off, it had become the Beacon. Either way, he thought, it shone a light in the vast prairie. And at his urging, his wife had resurrected the women's circles.

But he was at the stage of life where he was at the end of the beginning or the beginning of the end. Most likely the latter, he mused, as he drove into the countryside as the sun began to set. He had just discovered that he was going to eventually die after all, and that fact unnerved him. He had an awful feeling of dread.

> *He was* AT THE STAGE OF LIFE WHERE HE WAS AT THE END OF THE BEGINNING OR THE BEGINNING OF THE END.

Like his idol, young Teddy Roosevelt in the early part of the century, the Minister had been intrigued by the possibility of rejuvenating fresh air and open spaces, so he had come west to go to college. He also held to an idea that arose in the 1870s that the Almighty intended the Americans to expand from their eastern territory to the west as a part of a Manifest Destiny.

Now it seemed that the only things he liked about the West and South Dakota were the prairie sunsets. But they made him sad. Each one became one less that he would see, for he was at that point in time, as the German philosopher Schopenhauer had noted, where one begins to count backward from death rather than forward from birth.

He was also (he admitted to himself) spiritually fatigued, a soul in search of a sanctuary. He was having a difficult time lately balancing reverence with belief. His original faith, a firm, beautiful light, was now filled with doubt.

He was not sure anymore whether God created us or we created Him. For how could one reconcile the existence of God and His New Testament love with the senseless death of the little child at the downtown playground last month? Was death "an infinite abyss," as Pascal had noted, or was the little boy now really standing before the Lord with all the hosts of heaven at his side, as he had told the grieving parents? He wished he understood more.

It was all too much, and his mind drifted as he drove through the undulating grass and sagebrush countryside. "What would happen if one of those new round bales of hay in the ditch got to rolling?" he said to himself. "How far would it go? How could you stop it?"

And then, as he turned off the gravel road into the lane to go to Lyle Grover's ranch, he wondered, *Why do I have the urge to moo as I drive past those cows?*

MEANWHILE, BACK AT THE MANSE

The Minister's Wife had prepared an evening meal of a big dish of scalloped potatoes and ham. It was a favorite of a guy who, like all Presbyterian ministers, was a noted trencherman. Most wives of the preachers who adhered to John Calvin's teachings had become used to the fact that their husbands had hearty appetites.

Devouring food was one of the things that made the Presbyterians, Presbyterian. Some said the natural penchant among the denomination's pastors was enhanced by their studies in "Eating 101," a course that was rumored to be a requirement in many Presbyterian seminaries. The Minister's Wife also planned to serve a big piece of peach pie to top off the meal. It might take the sting out of what she had to tell him.

The regular organist, Ada Garlow, had phoned and said she couldn't play this coming Sunday. Her arthritis was acting up, and it had hit her on the right wrist. That meant that Bessie Klinger would be at the instrument.

Bessie substituted whenever Ada couldn't be there, and her appearance at the organ on a Sunday morning was usually greeted with an audible sigh by most of the congregation. Some of the men tried unsuccessfully to stifle a groan and received a gentle elbow in the ribs from their wives.

For Bessie was bad. She seemed to know only one tempo for any hymn, a marchlike sixty beats a minute, which she pounded out in the chords made by her left hand. Unfortunately, her right hand couldn't keep up, and so while her left hand went onward with Christian precision (with the chords), her right hand (with the melody) was about a half a beat behind. The um-pa-pa effect of the afterbeats made "Holy, Holy, Holy" sound like a polka rendered by the Five Pudgy Polocks!

The Minister's Wife waited 'til after the meal to tell her husband the news about Ada so that he could enjoy his food. And he responded with the only phrase of annoyance she ever heard him utter. "Peach pits!" he said, as he pushed himself away from the table.

But he calmed down enough to watch a bit of television on their brand-new set, and as they were preparing for bed, she broached the subject of the possibility of the town constructing a new playground. "I phoned some of the girls in Ruth

Circle after our meeting," she said, "and some other people while I was making supper, and everybody seemed to think it was a good idea."

Her husband grunted an assent.

"But everybody says it's up to the Council and the Mayor, and I'm afraid to talk to him. Could you bring it up with him?" she asked.

"Sure," he said.

And they crawled into bed.

But when he awoke the next morning, spooned together with his wife, he barely remembered it as one of the chores he had to do someday.

AROUND TOWN

After his spouse reminded him for the third time, the Minister finally caught up with the Mayor one night in September at the football game between the Larks and the Ida Grove Longhorns. Because of decreasing enrollments, the two towns now fielded six-man teams. That variation had been invented by a teacher in little Chester, Nebraska, in 1934 and had spread rapidly throughout the Plains states.

It was designed to keep football in the little places in big spaces that didn't have the manpower to field eleven-man squads. The game continued to be popular because high-school football brought a community together. Everybody went to the games, even though many of the ladies of the town thought the sport was just a big boy's version of the little boy's playground staple—piling on. "They run up and down the field banging into each other and falling down, and I haven't got a clue as to what's going on," said one.

The six-man games, however, were wonderfully entertaining for the menfolk. Success depended on speed and quickness, not strength and weight. It was a wide-open contest in which little guys could excel. There were three players in the line and three in the backfield, and everybody was eligible to catch a pass. With only six opponents to elude, a fast little lad could often break one tackle and be in the clear. It made for a never-dull extravaganza, with scores up in the forties and higher for both sides.

The Minister found the Mayor with the bunch of guys who were following the action up and down the scraggly field under the tall electric lights. Because there were no bleachers, the group moved along with the play on the field from the sidelines.

He squeezed between the well-fed bellies and big-buckle belts to get close to the Mayor but wisely decided to wait until half-time before bringing up the subject of the playground. Neither school had a band, so there weren't any halftime exercises, and the score was already thirty-four to six in favor of the Longhorns. Across the field, the Ida Grove cheerleaders were mounting a yell extolling the virtues of their junior-high team—the Shorthorns—which, they taunted, was going to come out to play the entire second half because they were so far ahead.

"Two bits, four bits, six bits, a dollar! All for the Shorthorns stand up and holler!" they yelled. The folks on the Grand Meadow sidelines studiously ignored them.

The Minister sidled up and explained the idea of, and the need for, a new playground, and the Mayor listened patiently. His reply, however, was uncommonly brief.

"Nope," he said, "the town can't afford it. We got all sorts of other priorities to take care of first."

This was true, but what the Minister didn't know was that he was the wrong one to plead any cause before the Mayor. Although it wasn't the case, the Mayor believed that the Minister had been one of his wife's boyfriends when they had both attended USD a few years back!

MEANWHILE, BACK AT THE MANSE

When Connie heard about her husband's turndown of the proposal at the next session of the Ruth Circle, she suspected the real reason behind the refusal. George had become more jealous lately. And more amorous. Maybe it was the change in the drinking water. The town had installed a new water system last year, and the stuff tasted sorta funny now. The Mayor was being held responsible.

The Minister's Wife, however, pressed the group to continue to consider the project. "We need this playground for our kids next summer," she said. And since there were seven kids among the four mothers present, everybody seemed to agree.

Myrtle was, of course, childless and tried to change the subject with her new gossip. It *was* old Widow Thompson who had lost the money at Needrow's Drug, she said. And Mable Johnson and Rick Rattery had been caught fiddle-faddlin' a little bit under the trees in the cemetery by the town marshal's flashlight.

"And did you hear about old Charlie Delperdang?" she continued. "He showed his Black Angus at the state fair in Huron and won Grand Champion honors. Then he went out and got tipsy at the Prairie Moon outside of town on the road to Wolsey and wrecked his car!"

The Prairie Moon was unique even for South Dakota, she admitted. One half of it was a club and restaurant and the other half a chicken hatchery. "You can be sure that your chicken dinner is fresh, even though those birds do make a lot of noise while you're eating," Myrtle chortled.

The Minister's Wife pressed on, pointedly ignoring the gossip, her resolve masked behind a polite smile. "We need a new place for our kids to play," she said determinedly.

Just last week her older boy had challenged the younger one to crawl into a concrete culvert beneath the Great Northern railway tracks while a train passed over. The little one had chickened out, began to run, straightened up, and cut his head open. The older one had used his dirty handkerchief and the sewer water to wash out the wound and (afraid of the retribution to come) took him only to the corner, a block away from the Manse. The little guy staggered the rest of the way, clutching the snotty handkerchief to his bleeding head. The Minister's Wife had rushed him to the doctor, and a series of shots and stitches saved the day.

Later, taking advantage of the turbanlike bandage, the older one took his little brother around the neighborhood and told all the little girls that his brother had been operated on and had his brains taken out. The little fella acted the part with suitable grunts and a rolling of the eyes, jerking of the head, and dribbling of the mouth. The horrified little girls fled home to their mothers.

"We need someplace for our kids to play safely," The Minister's Wife repeated. And she reminded them of the tragedy of the little boy at the old playground earlier that year.

"Maybe we need to ascertain just how much a new playground will cost," said Pauline, eyelashes aflutter. "If the Mayor and the Council knew the exact figure of the proposed expenditure, maybe they could find the wherewithal in the budget."

Everybody nodded in agreement. And that's how Pauline's cousin got into the act.

AROUND TOWN

He was the Director of Parks and Recreation in Rapid City, and he agreed to come out to Grand Meadow and work up an estimate for a new playground on one condition: that Pauline would bake him one of her famous pumpkin chiffon pies. There'd be no charge for the estimate, just a coupla'—maybe three—pieces of pie. And some coffee to wash 'em down. And—oh yeah—she had to promise not to use that highfalutin language on him.

There was only one problem. Pauline was short of pumpkins. Someone kept getting into her patch.

It had become so annoying that she had taken out a classified ad addressed TO WHOM IT MAY CONCERN in the *Bugle* that week. She promised to give the thief free pumpkins if he'd just ask for them nicely.

But she calculated that she would have enough to make her cousin a pie or two, and so a deal was struck. Her relative said he'd be over the next week.

True to his word, he showed up, and Pauline took him down to the little park with the old playground equipment. After some squatting and squinting and measuring and figuring and scratching of the head, he said he thought he had it about right, and they went back to Pauline's kitchen for the pie.

Between mouthfuls, he wrote down his estimates and explained them to Pauline. They'd have to throw out the old equipment and put some pipes in for drainage when it rained or snowed, he said. And then they'd need to do some grading and leveling and sanding. They could then install new playground equipment, and he sketched out a rough plan. They'd have two slides for bigger and smaller kids, a wooden tunnel for them to crawl through (and on), a big new swing set, a teetertotter, and a low thing that went 'round and 'round like a merry-go-round. And to top it all off, a big jungle gym that all the kids could climb up and about on!

It would cost between three and five thousand dollars, depending on whether they got top-of-the-line equipment that would last forever (almost), he said. And they could save some on labor if volunteers worked on the project under (he stressed) "professional supervision."

After her cousin left, Pauline ran over to the Manse and gave the estimates to The Minister's Wife.

That lady was delighted with them, particularly with the possibility of getting a wooden tunnel for kids to crawl in and out of.

And that night she showed them to her husband and asked him to take them to the Mayor. But the parson seemed preoccupied and merely grunted when she tried to hand them to him. Clearly he had lost whatever little interest he had in the project.

The Minister was deep into his own thoughts at the time. For while he was becoming used to the idea of his own mortality, he was also becoming aware that his life would probably end on a minor chord. *What am I doing in this nowhere place doing nothing things?* he kept asking himself. *Who am I? Why don't I understand more?*

He was still struggling with his floundering faith and beginning to experience John Cheever's three worlds of day, night, and the night within the night. He was seeing his moonlit shadow on the lawn at 2:00 a.m. too many times lately.

But he finally bestirred himself back to the moment, accepted the playground estimates from his wife, and said he'd do what he could. "Soon," he promised.

Two days later the Minister found the Mayor down at the stockyards by the train depot. His Honor was there politicking with the ranchers and hands from the nearby spreads, who had brought in loads of cattle for shipment to the packing plants in Sioux Falls.

Between the brays and bellows of the animals and the shouts and curses of the cowhands as they moved them into the pens, the Minister managed to get the estimates into the Mayor's hand. But it did no good.

Shouting above the din, the Mayor explained his position once more, without even looking at the papers. He was brief and to the point. "Look, Reverend," he hollered. "It don't matter whether it's five thousand or five hundred dollars! We can't afford it!" And that, at least for the time being, was that!

MEANWHILE, BACK AT THE MANSE

Some of the ladies at the next meeting of the Ruth Circle thought they had it all figured out when they heard that the Mayor had turned the idea down again. It's because of his background, they said to themselves. For George was a lapsed Catholic.

He had spent his early years in nearby Ida Grove and had attended Our Lady of the Holy Nativity, which the Protestants in Grand Meadow had dubbed Our Lady of Perpetual Activity, when they weren't referring to its Immaculate Kitchen. There seemed to be a bingo game or something else happening over there every night.

But George was now what some folks called an A-and-P Catholic. He usually only showed up for Mass on Ash Wednesday and Palm Sunday.

The people at the Good News Gospel Church back home thought that he probably wasn't even a Christian. He had once been heard to quip that he distrusted people who had found the Lord. "Where was He hiding?" he laughed.

Even some OF HIS CATHOLIC FRIENDS SAID THAT HE PROBABLY THOUGHT THAT GOOD FRIDAY RUINED AN OTHERWISE PERFECTLY GOOD WEEKEND.

And then there was this thing about "God's will." "Where was it, and who was going to read it?" he joked. Even some of his Catholic friends said that he probably thought that Good Friday ruined an otherwise perfectly good weekend.

George also held a dim view of most religious leaders, for he thought they were merely professional optimists who believed that every jerk in the world was simply a saint waiting to be discovered. And he often said so.

So maybe the problem was in who was presenting the idea rather than the idea itself, thought some of the ladies. Maybe if somebody other than a Man of God approached him, they'd have more luck. "Maybe we'll have to undertake this task ourselves," said Pauline, wrinkling up her nose.

And to take the sting out of their disappointment over the turndown, she passed out some tiny sample vials of her newly discovered fragrance—Lacy Passion—that she had picked up at Needrow's Drug the day before. She also told them about a new aftershave cologne called Aqua Velva. She had bought a bottle for Doc because she had heard that some of the wives on the ranches he served with his veterinary skills had begun flirting with him. "That stuff is so pungent," she said, "that it could wipe out the entire female population of South Dakota!"

Dippy Mickie also tried to lift everyone's spirits by announcing that she was up to four mallets on her xylophone now, and had learned to play "He's Just My Bill" from *Show Boat*. She was going to serenade her husband with it after supper that night. She'd be accompanied by her mother on the accordion.

Myrtle jumped in with some new gossip about Mrs. Stopplemyer, who was having "female troubles." This general phrase covered a multitude of medical problems, and its utterance was always accompanied by—and greeted with—lifted eyebrows and shared and knowing glances among the ladies. The specifics of the case were as mysterious as those of the females who had suffered from "the vapors" in Victorian days. The details were too intimate for anyone to share—sometimes even with a lady's own doctor.

But The Minister's Wife was agitated—and yes—even annoyed by the Mayor's turndown and bent upon keeping the subject of the playground in front of the minds of her fellow church members. So she interrupted the silent speculations about the specific malady that had laid Mrs. Stopplemyer low by quietly demanding, "We have got to get this planned so we have it next summer! We must get some support for the playground project!"

"What if we devised a petition?" queried Pauline in her most important-sounding voice. "We could compose one right now and circulate it to ascertain its efficacy, and if we acquire enough signatures, the Mayor and the Council will have to at least take it under consideration."

"And we kin have it at ar church booth at tha rodeo nex' week an git ever'body who comes by ta sign it," said Mickie. "We'll make those guys lissen ta us!"

AROUND TOWN

The rodeo was a once-a-year event held in a corral at the edge of town in late fall as the few leaves were turning. It was officially called the Grand Meadow Rodeo and Live Stock Exhibition. The two-day attraction was sponsored by the Better Grand Meadow Club and was designed to bring business into the community before the bitter winter snows set in.

It did. Folks came from miles around, as the saying went, to watch brave cowpokes (or foolish ones, depending on your point of view) get thrown, gored, kicked, pawed, and stomped on by two thousand pounds of slashing hooves, horns, and muscle. Or to watch them try to survive the frenzied bucking of a wild horse for a few seconds, or perhaps rope and hogtie a calf.

When they weren't watching the chutes open and the sight of guys trying desperately to control the wild-eyed beasts (or at least survive the encounter), the spectators could visit the many vendors of Western paraphernalia that were set up near the rodeo site. Hats, boots, string ties, and the like were for sale. If they got hungry or thirsty (what with all the dust), they could stop by one of the church stands for a "Cool Beverage," as the signs always promised. And maybe a piece of pie.

The Presbyterian stand was set up right opposite the one operated by the Lutherans, and it vied with them for patrons.

Each competed with the other every year in coming up with a gimmick that would pull in the customers.

This year the Presbyterians set up a big Mason jar full of corn kernels at the front of the stand. The person who came the closest to estimating the number of kernels in the jar got a tasty loose-meat sandwich (a "Tavern"), with a large drink, some delicious coleslaw, potato salad and, of course, an extra big piece of apple pie. Free!

Such things didn't really bring in trade that much, though, according to most observers. Folks usually patronized the stand of the church where they were members or where their relatives or friends went. In either place, they knew they were going to get some good food, cooked by some very good cooks.

The Presbyterians had their playground petition at the stand as an added inducement. The ladies of Ruth Circle manned the pencils and even called out to passersby in a most un-Presbyterian fashion. "Sign up for a new playground!" they implored in loud but gentle voices.

And people responded. By the time of the traditional closing-night "Single vs. Married Men Softball Game on Donkeys" at the ball diamond, Ruth Circle had collected more than ninety names!

Led by The Minister's Wife, the five members of Ruth Circle marched right over to the Mayor and presented him with the signed petitions. He was sitting on the fender of his car off to one side of third base at the time and, seeing his wife in the group, he wisely decided to accept the papers. He promised to "consult with the Council on the matter." Most everybody—except the ladies—knew that "consultation" (in the Mayor's definition) meant that, in the words of Ambrose

Bierce, he would "seek another approval of a course already decided upon."

MEANWHILE, BACK AT THE MANSE

The Council took its own sweet time in coming to a determination, and it was early January before word spread about the Council's turndown of the petition. The members of Ruth Circle pulled on their overshoes and drove hurriedly through the snowy streets to the Manse, even though there was no scheduled meeting. They were indignant!

"How dare that collection of cretins ignore us?" Pauline said passionately in her nose-in-the-air manner. "They are simply not listening and adhering to the will and desires of the populace!" she huffed.

"Where da they cum off with this kinda stuff?" cried Mickie, bursting into tears. "Who da they thank we are?"

She had been crying a lot lately, anyhow. Maybe it was the length of the cold white winter, but she was becoming dismayed about her role as a woman. Bill didn't seem to appreciate her or her xylophone playing very much anymore. Or maybe it was the consciousness-raising article she had read in one of the women's magazines at the beauty parlor. It had talked about "finding oneself." Or maybe she was crying because just when she was beginning to think of herself as a guest star on the new Lawrence Welk TV show, an incident had brought her back to earth and to her role in life in this lonesome place.

Just yesterday, during the brief warm spell (she told the ladies between sobs), she had left her kids with a sitter while she went grocery shopping. When she came out of Top's Market, she found that she had locked her keys in the car.

She phoned Bill, who was in an "important meeting" with the Mayor and some guys from the pipe company about why the town's water tasted so bad. Could he come over and unlock the car with his extra set of keys?

"Can't you wait?" he had asked.

"No!" she had replied. "The sitter's gotta go ta cheerleadin' practice."

So, grumbling and irritated, Bill said he'd come over.

But while she leaned against the car waiting for him, she noticed that one of the back windows was wide open! "What'd you do?" someone gasped!

"What would YOU do?" sobbed Mickie. "Ah reached in, opened tha doah, rolled up that winder, locked up tha doah agin, an' waited fer Bill." The ladies of Ruth Circle rushed to embrace her with warm sympathy.

After the hugs all 'round, the talk turned back to the Council and the playground project. "My momma done tole me that sometimes tha way ta get a guy ta do somethin' is ta tell him he's too old ta do it," said Mickie, between sniffles. "Maybe if we . . ."

But she was cut off by Myrtle, The Man-and-Council Basher. "They're all a bunch of sourpusses over there anyhow," she said angrily. "Maybe the reason they're so unhappy as men is that there's so little chance for advancement! Perhaps we ought to set up a men's correctional facility," she continued. "Maybe we could construct it as an adjunct to the prison the state is proposing over in Ida Grove. We could send the really dumb ones there for a specified length of time."

But as The Minister's Wife poured the coffee for them around the kitchen table, the group lapsed into thought. Their heads were down. There seemed to be so little they could do to change the situation.

Pretentious Pauline finally broke the silence. "Remember when we were engaging in a bit of humor about how men could be trained like dogs?" she mused aloud.

There were nods and some smiles.

"But seriously," she went on in her la-de-da manner, "dogs are conditioned to alter and modify their behavior—why not men? Dogs like food treats and so do men. Promise them what they want if they perform as they should." And as she warmed to the idea and straightened up, she grew more enthusiastic, "Maybe even make them beg a little," she giggled. "They'll acquiesce and come around to seeing things our way."

Eyebrows—then heads—were raised.

"Ya mean . . . ?" gasped Mickie.

Pauline nodded.

And then Connie spoke up.

She had been quietly furious with her husband's treatment of this issue, and although she usually never interfered with his official mayoral determinations, this was getting ridiculous! Besides, the Minister had NOT been one of her boyfriends in college; he had been one of the few she hadn't gone out with! So she figured she owed him—and his wife—one. If they were for this, then she was for this! Besides, she had two kids who could use the playground.

Maybe ol' snooty Pauline had an idea there, she thought. Maybe food could be used as a weapon. Maybe they could manipulate. She had learned the hard way that withholding something was the best weapon a woman could have in her arsenal.

And what's more elemental even than love? What's more important to a man—lovin' or food?

Except for air and water, what's more essential? FOOD! These guys liked to eat. Man, did they like to eat! They gobbled it down! They devoured it! They had appetites that wouldn't quit! Maybe they could ladle out good food in miserly doses until they got the playground. So she mentally ticked off the potential targets.

There was her George, the Mayor, of course, and she could put out small portions of food for him. And pretentious Pauline's brother-in-law was on the City Council. Pauline's husband, Doc, would put the pressure on him, after he got some pressure himself from Pauline, in the form of little dollops of food. Mickie's Bill was employed by the Council and could talk to them if he got hungry enough. There was the Minister (and his Presbyterian appetite) who needed some further motivation to pursue the issue with the Mayor. The Minister's Wife would handle that.

Myrtle was single and didn't have anybody to ration food to, but she'd sure be with them in spirit, and maybe they could get some of the members of their sister group—the Martha Circle—to go along with it. And then who knows?

"Look, since a dog is at his best when he wants to be fed, we ought to keep the bowl half full so he always wants more," Connie said. "We can keep them in constant hunger until they see things our way."

Myrtle upped the ante. "Why not TOTAL hunger until they come around?" she asked with fire in her voice.

"Ya mean . . . ?" asked Mickie.

Could they? Should they? Would they? They all looked at one another. And the pureness of the strategy came upon them!

"YESSS! YESSS!" cried Connie. "We'll become like Aristophanes's *Lysistrata*!" remembering her old Greek literature class at USD. "But instead of no more lovin' from the women until the men stopped warring, it'll be NO MORE COOKING FROM US UNTIL WE GET THE PLAYGROUND!"

Maybe it was a lifetime of being dominated by, and terribly dependent on, an immense and endless land where the horizon was a constant presence and geography was destiny. Maybe it was always being looked down on and taken for granted by sad-eyed taciturn men who used a lot of silence when they talked, and who were cut off by temperament and environment from the outside world. Maybe it was just the feminine unity created by Mickie's recent car keys incident.

Whatever it was, the ladies of Ruth Circle nodded defiantly to each other in a moment of fierce determination. By golly, they'd do it!

"STARTING TONIGHT!" cried Connie.

"Who's Aristophane and what's a *Lysistrata?*" asked Mickie. Nobody answered her, but she moved to join hands with the rest of them in a silent but emphatic gesture of solidarity.

The Minister's Wife was a bit hesitant. Not that they were going to become the Ruth Circle Knitting and Terrorist Society, but this was—this was—well—Presbyterian heresy! No more cooking? A hungry husband? What would the consequences be? Would she be drummed out of the church? But she quietly shook her head in defiance and joined the group.

And as they withdrew their hands, she summoned up some words that put the plot to convince the Council in a somewhat more gentle way. She had been reading a biography of Abraham Lincoln and, borrowing a phrase from that great man, she murmured, "Perhaps in this way we can help them all locate the better angel of their nature."

Meanwhile, *Back at the* Manse

AROUND TOWN

Connie took charge as usual and did indeed convince some of the ladies of the Martha Circle to join in, even though they ordinarily followed the biblical description of their namesake, who had been "distracted with much serving." And she went around town talking forcefully with many nonchurch members. Her position as the wife of the Mayor made the cause "most interesting," said some.

And many of the other white-bread Protestant ladies and bridge clubs in Grand Meadow linked up with the Presbyterian women. "It's about time we stand up for what WE want with those guys," some said. It was as if they were beginning to feel that a man in a woman's life was not her MANIFEST DESTINY.

The crusade also reached the ladies out on the lonely ranches surrounding Grand Meadow. Word circulated largely due to Connie's use of the rural party telephone line. A few calls to Ottie Nelson (who was even more gossipy that Myrtle) spread the word, because most of the rural housewives picked up their receivers and listened in eagerly whenever Ottie's "three shorts and a long" rang down the line.

The women's tactics were remarkably similar. At first it was, "Sorry, I didn't have time to cook for you today. I have a headache." When that malady seemed to persist, concerned questions were raised by the guys about their wives' health. Husbands began to become downright solicitous. Needrow's Drug had a run on aspirin.

But that didn't seem to alleviate the problem or make any difference, and of course, the wives did cook—somewhat. They prepared meals for themselves and their children, if they had any. The portions were smaller and were served with paper napkins and knives and forks. But they set no place for their husbands at the table, and so the guys had to fend for themselves.

And eventually the wives began to tell their husbands the reason for their actions. The guys were dumbfounded! "All this for a playground?" seemed to be the universal reaction.

So at first, some of the good ole boys tried to soldier on— defiantly. Instead of a hearty portion of bacon and eggs and hash browns for breakfast, they settled for some cold cereal and poured milk on it. Luncheon sandwiches were made by slapping some bologna between two slices of bread. Forget lettuce.

For supper, some hot dogs or even a steak over the barbeque out back, even in the blustery winter, seemed adventuresome. "I'll show her!" they seemed to say.

But the steaks were expensive, and a diet of hamburger and hot dogs lost its magic after a while. Anyhow, it was really too cold out there to barbeque with any regularity. Bundling up in snow boots and parkas to cook soon lost its charm.

And the "things" that accompanied meat were a mystery. None of the guys had ever taken the home-economics course from the legendary Mrs. Hammer during their Grand Meadow High School days. She had taught her girl charges that every meal should be balanced by color. Under her scheme, one should have yellows, reds, greens, and browns for a wholesome meal. A nutritious repast might consist of corn (yellow) and a lettuce salad (green) to accompany the meat (brown) all topped off by a cherry pie (red).

This concept and menu was completely beyond the capabilities of any South Dakota cowboy. None even had a clue as to how to make those masculine delights—potato salad or coleslaw, although rumor had it that both involved mayonnaise. And the folks over at that Hold-the-Mayo-Clinic in Rochester, Minnesota were beginning to say that stuff was bad for you.

When they were finally driven inside the house, there were those new "heat and serve" meals that one could now get at Top's Market. After they finally figured out the controls, the fellas used the oven after the rest of the family had finished their supper. But the stuff in the package got all squished together instead of staying in its place in the little compartments, and what didn't burn was pretty tasteless. No amount of ketchup could hide that fact.

So a lot of the guys resorted to opening cans of something and heating them up on the stove after their wife and kids left the kitchen. But most of the stuff was bland and got monotonous. There was little variety and no different taste to any slapped-together meal. And of course that ultimate in male culinary delights on the northern prairie, a piece of pie, was impossible to even contemplate making. No guy had the skills or patience.

The parson at the Good News Gospel Church seized the opportunity created by the guys' dilemma and advised the menfolk that they should adopt the Mediterranean diet of two thousand years ago. "Try eating what Jesus ate," he said. But that was a simple meal of bread, olive oil, and wine.

Eventually SOME OF THE GUYS BEGAN TO FEEL THAT THIS DEPRIVATION OF GOOD FOOD WAS BUT A CONTINUATION OF THE LUCK IN THE SAD SPECTACLE OF THEIR LIVES.

Where would a person get olive oil out here in South Dakota? And wine? That was a girl's drink.

The parson over at St. Paul's Lutheran went his colleague one better by suggesting that they try *entomophagy*—the eating of bugs. "After all," he said, "John the Baptist did eat locusts and wild honey." Wait until spring when there were sure to be a lot of grasshoppers out on the prairie. "Try 'em," he said. "Ugh" was the usual reaction.

The Minister at First Presbyterian was silent on the matter. His wife was one of the ringleaders in this revolt, and things were a bit strained around the house already. *Best be quiet*, he thought.

With little religious leadership, one would have thought the fellas would have fought back somehow by banding together. But there was no collective will, mainly because the guys didn't really talk to one another about it. It was one thing to ask a parson for suggestions. There was confidentiality about that. But another guy?

The subject was too embarrassing. Macho pride was at stake

here. A few wives hadn't joined the boycott, and who knew just who was being subjected to it? No fella dared admit to not being in control of his own house.

And there were few men's organizations comparable to the many ladies' groups where they could talk about it. Oh, there were the occasional meetings of the Better Grand Meadow Club, of course, and the monthly meetings of the Elks. But they had fourteen and seventeen members respectively, and a dude couldn't reveal his status in that big a group.

Some of the guys sang in the men's community singing group called the O.K. Chorale, whose bass-dominated harmonics led one lady critic to call it the Drone on the Range—although she admitted that they weren't as bad as they sounded. But that group was also not the place to own up to their dilemma.

Eventually some of the guys began to feel that this deprivation of good food was but a continuation of the bad luck in the sad spectacle of their lives. They began to come around to thinking that they probably deserved it.

There WAS the morning coffee group, the ROMEOs (Retired Old Men Eating Out), as they called themselves, who did share their dire situation among themselves. Five or six old boys usually met at Clara's Coffee Corner along about nine o'clock to drink some of the steamin' stuff and shoot the breeze at a table in the back.

They usually tossed dice in a cup to see who paid for the brew, except when a stranger was brought to the table. Then they straightened up and made a motion and elected him president of the ROMEOs. He was usually so honored that only later did he realize that the sole duty of the office was to pay for the coffee and maybe a piece of pie. After a good laugh, they all wandered off to do whatever it was they thought they had to do.

Clara's was a family restaurant, even though she had once

pasted a notice inside the front door that warned, Unattended children will be sold as slaves. Her place was the only eatery in town, and during the first week or so of the no-cooking campaign, she had a rush of business.

But she was a widow lady who had been left a good pension, and the only reason she kept the café open was in memory of her husband, who had named the place after her. It was more of a habit than anything else now, and so she finally caved in to the blandishments of the ladies in town.

One day a notice chalked on the daily special sign in the window announced a new menu: *Closed—Until—Whenever.* The ROMEOs slunk away.

It got colder. And even the winter boredom that was occasionally relieved by driving through ten feet of snow and 30 mph winds to attend a high-school basketball tournament didn't relieve the guys' appetites. The towns were small and had no restaurants, and the only thing served at the local gym was popcorn.

So as the weeks turned into two months, a sort of silence settled on Grand Meadow. The guys grew hungrier, and the ladies grew their hair long and wore nylon stockings to their meetings ("to keep out the cold," they said). And they began to have just a bit of a smug look on their faces.

So by the time the snow got to melting and patches of earth began to appear and a fella was maybe thinking about taking the storm windows off, there were some mad old boys around town and some strange behavior. The boycott had really begun to have an impact!

The Minister seemed to be particularly affected. Lately he had been questioning himself even more. "Who am I?" he kept saying to the mirror as he shaved. "Why don't I understand more?"

Maybe, he thought, *the too-examined life is not worth living.*

But lately he had found himself pondering the age-old question, "Did Adam and Eve have belly buttons?" After all, they didn't have a mother.

And this food protest was ridiculous. A Calvinist appetite was a given thing. Presbyterians loved food. But to have to cook the food he devoured was—well—unseemly! It took the joy out of eating—and out of life.

He had also become persuaded that the services at First Presbyterian were boring. The same thing went on Sunday after Sunday. There was an introit, the call to worship, the Scripture reading, the sermon, the prayers, the offertory, et cetera, et cetera, all in the same order each Sunday.

So at a meeting of the local governing body—the session—he suggested that maybe they should try to hold services something like an Orthodox Jewish *shul*. There'd be tallithim and a parade of the Bible and exotic smells. It would all be seemingly impromptu. People could arrive at any time they wanted to, join the readings of the Scripture, mosey about and say hello to other folk, and rejoin the readings. And when they felt they had enough or wanted to leave, they could go.

There would be no sermon. "It would make the strange familiar and the familiar strange," he said.

The members of the session looked at one another. *This food deprivation thing has really gotten to the Minister*, they thought. *The lack of good and sufficient food has affected his brain. You never—but never—try to change the order of worship in a local Presbyterian church!* Even a first-year seminary student knew that!

The boycott had gotten to the Mayor too. George was simply not his ebullient and loquacious self these days. He had become quieter and had lost some weight.

He had also become a bit testy; one day he yelled at his secretary in a most unprofessional way. He was perpetually hungry and couldn't concentrate on his insurance sales or the town's business. And fellas kept coming up to him and whispering, "Give 'em the playground, for God's sake!"

So he determined to do just that. The winter's snowstorms had been lighter than expected, and the Council hadn't spent all they had set aside to plow the streets. They'd use that and some of the money they were saving for the rescue unit.

So the Mayor set out up the street to tell the Minister about his decision.

The two met at the corner of Main and Maple, for the good Reverend had determined to make another stab at convincing George of the necessity of the playground project and was headed downtown to confront His Honor at the little city hall.

When the Mayor told him of his decision, the Minister smiled with a joy he hadn't felt in months. A major burden had been lifted!

Things were going to get better! Buds were appearing on the trees! Spring was here! The air had lost its chilly edge and now, so would his wife! A passage from the Song of Solomon popped into his head: *Comfort me with apples: for I am sick of love.* Food, glorious food, was on the way!

And after the sudden resolution of this playground problem, his other difficulties suddenly seemed more manageable. Perhaps the uncertainties and confusion he had been granted by God was a tiny part of The Truth and about as much understanding as we mere mortals were ever going to get. Maybe we are given only such understanding as is sufficient for each of us. Maybe, like St.

Anselm maintained, "*Credo et intelligam*" (I [should] believe in order that I understand).

Closer to home, maybe it all was like the philosophy of the Lakota Sioux, who had occupied this vast South Dakota prairie for centuries. Maybe there was only—The Great Mystery.

And who was he? Maybe he was just like that great spinach-eating philosopher—Popeye—in the funny papers. "I yam what I yam," he said to himself. No more, no less. And in a terribly un-Presbyterian manner the Minister kicked up his heels as he rounded the corner to the Manse!

When the word spread around town and into the countryside about the Mayor's capitulation, there was great rejoicing and a lot of "Yee-hawin'!" by the guys. If they would have had pistols, there would sure as the Devil been a lot of holes shot in the early spring sky THAT day!

Most of the wives laid on a big banquet in their homes that night. They prepared their husband's favorite meal. And the guys chowed down! BIG TIME!

MEANWHILE, BACK AT THE MANSE

When her husband told her the good news, The Minister's Wife smiled quietly and began to prepare a big Presbyterian supper for him. She wasn't surprised. The strategy had been bound to work, and she'd known they'd get the playground eventually.

So lately she had been thinking. What the kids and this town really needed was a swimming pool. What was that *Lysistrata* thing about again?

The
Eleventh
Commandment

The further decoding of some previously unreadable fragments of the Dead Sea Scrolls has revealed—an Eleventh
Commandment! Or so say some biblical scholars.

The two-thousand-year-old scrolls were unearthed between
1947 and 1956 in caves near the Dead Sea. Their discovery
touched off a series of major debates among theologians about
their implications for Jewish as well as Christian beliefs.

Because the initial study of the scrolls was limited to a very
few academicians, suspicions arose that some of the translations
were being suppressed by (among others) the Roman Catholic
Church, because they would undermine some long-established
dogma of ancient times concerning the origins of Christianity.
Some folk even nurtured the idea that the manuscripts held
darker secrets.

In the past few years, the study of the scrolls has been

opened to more scholars and, indeed, new insights have been found from the eight hundred texts contained in them. Infrared technology has been used to read some of the writings on the smaller fragments. And the study of the precious documents by more people has resulted in more interpretations of the writings.

No bombshells have appeared, just new perceptions. But now two scholars from the University of Okoboji in Milford, Iowa, have made the astonishing discovery that one of the scrolls contains a version of what they are calling the Eleventh Commandment!

That scroll apparently has some writing on it that is an early

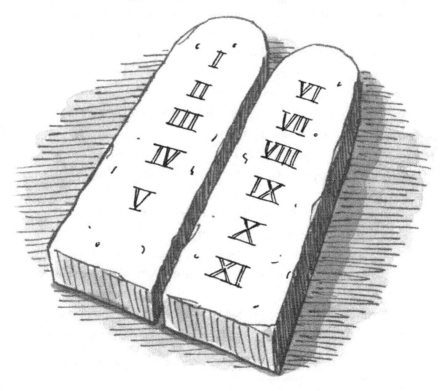

version of the well-known ten divine commands and prohibitions that were handed down to Moses on Mount Sinai. Portions of admonitions and warnings about graven images, adultery, stealing, and the like are all there.

But there is also one more commandment—an Eleventh! The academics, however, are divided as to its exact translation. One professor believes it should be deciphered as "Thou Shalt Laugh." The other thinks the translation should be in the negative—"Thou Shalt NOT Laugh."

Unto itself, the latter interpretation would not be enough for the Vatican to have tried to suppress the document. After all, in addition to their self-confessed inability to sing, Roman Catholics are not usually known for their great sense of humor. So Catholics would presumably agree with a command from on high that one should not laugh.

But an acknowledgment of a negative interpretation of the new commandment would also put them in concert with what many folk consider to be the most humorless of all the Protestant denominations—the Presbyterians.[1]

Some people say that such ecumenical agreement on such an important aspect of the human condition could possibly be dangerous.

As many folks know, the dour Calvinists are usually not known to be a joyous lot under any circumstances. We often seem to operate in a humor-free zone. A member of our denomination is said to be ever on guard against levity, for a laugh may be fatal.

For a Presbyterian to be happy, there probably should be an aura of cloudiness surrounding everything. A few physicians, of

---

1. Because the author of this book is a staunch Presbyterian, he believes he has an obligation to point out the follies and foibles of his wonderful denomination.

other faiths, of course, say that the Presbyterians seem to suffer from a medical condition known as anhedonia—the incapacity to experience happiness.

The tone was presumably set by the founder of the denomination, John Calvin, in the 1500s in Geneva, Switzerland. This theologian saw to it that the city fathers passed civil laws against drunkenness, adultery, debauchery, and profanity. They also banned playing cards, dancing (even in one's home), and any manner of "worldly dress." Babies' names were restricted to those in the Bible, and children could be imprisoned for lying.

The strait-laced Calvin was said to have put a man in jail for laughing in church. And some reports have it that he often woke up in the middle of the night, worrying that somewhere in the world, someone was having a good time.

The cleric's most controversial belief, however, was in predestination. The beak-nosed intellectual maintained that even before the Creation, God chose (or elected) only some for faith. Salvation was not to be earned but is a gift, and certain folks will receive the gift and others reject it.

This belief later caused all sorts of interpretations and much discussion within the Presbyterian denomination, with no definitive understanding of the doctrine. A lot of current members of the church have no opinion about predestination one way or the other, and many have never even heard of it.

But after this basic theology was promulgated, many of Calvin's followers failed to advance in philosophical thought. They are said to have adopted the idea that progress was all right as long as it didn't change anything. And in later years, some of the members of other denominations began calling Presbyterians "the Frozen Chosen" because of some of our seemingly inflexible traditions and supposed belief in predestination.

One of Calvin's fervent disciples was the Scot, John Knox. He cranked up the zeal of the denomination another notch with his thundering rhetoric against sin and sloth. From behind a thin beard that stretched below his waist, he condemned and censured all who failed to conform to his beliefs.

Like Calvin, he emphasized the negatives in life. Some said he was mad because when he was young, he was so skinny that they used him to clean out the cannons. Others said he always had a bit of a frown on his face because his underwear was too tight.

Calvin died in 1564 and Knox in 1572. There is no record of either smiling during his lifetime.

Today, Presbyterians are a bit more relaxed about things. Some women of our denomination are now said to display their displeasure at something by quietly knitting faster, and they even answer the phone on the first ring. But they supposedly still don't trust anybody who does her own hair, and many still carry handkerchiefs in their sleeves.

Presbyterian men are also somewhat less rigid today, although some of us are still of the belief that *Naughty Marietta* was an adult film, and many are still a bit concerned about what made *The Merry Widow* merry. To a few, the Boston Pops is considered a jazz band, and "Rock of Ages" is as close to modern music as they want to get!

And many of the men and women of the denomination resolutely stick to one of the austere beliefs of our founders: It is a SIN to have a sense of humor. Life is SERIOUS! One should never laugh.

The tone, of course, is set by the local minister. And, according to Presbyterian protocol, all candidates for that job must be carefully examined for evidence of any funny stuff in their background.

To ignore this detail is to be seen as courting disaster. It may even bring on a calamity, such as that which occurred in a small Presbyterian church in Ohio in the mid-1980s.

There the Pastoral Nominating Committee (PNC) recommended, and the congregation hired, a young man with impeccable credentials who possessed a demeanor of sanctimonious piety. They neglected to discover, however, that even on days as bad as a rained-out ball game, he had been seen to smile.

For the first month or so, things went swimmingly. But then the New Pastor began to lose it. He had a sense of humor—and a rather bizarre one, at that!

It became evident with his reading of the Scriptures at the Sunday morning worship services. Normally, he read ponderously but with great feeling. However, on one sunny morning, for unknown reasons, he began to dissolve into uncontrollable laughter as he read through that day's text.

It started with a slight upturn on the right side of his mouth, which he covered with his hand. Between long pauses and deep breaths, a series of s-s-s-s's escaped from his pursed lips as he fought to control himself. With his hand over his mouth, his speech became somewhat unintelligible, and this seemed to exacerbate things. A giggle or two escaped, and tears began to well up in his eyes.

A laugh was building and working its way to the surface, and in an effort to suppress it, he hunched over with his hands on the pulpit, and his shoulders began to shake. But it was all to no avail, as he finally erupted in a barked *"Har! Har! Har!"* just as he finished the reading and sat down.

The congregation was stunned. They looked at one another. It was all decidedly un-Presbyterian.

The Minister apologized to the Chairman of the Worship Committee at the coffee hour, and people shrugged off the incident. But it began to happen with more frequency on subsequent Sundays.

It usually started somewhere near the middle of the Young Minister's reading of the Scriptures. A grin would bring on a giggle, and the giggle would bring on a chuckle. In an effort to restore some solemnity, he would lower his voice an octave,

wrinkle his brow, and adopt a superserious mien. His hand would go to his face, and he would bite his lips in an attempt to stifle the forthcoming laugh.

And in a frantic tactic to get through the reading before he lost control, he would pick up the pace, making the partially smothered words even more incomprehensible. On some occasions, he made it to the end before he collapsed back into his chair beside the pulpit, with great whoops of delight!

But on some Sundays, after a gallant battle, he would surrender to his own merriment during the reading, and it would have to be abandoned.

The Pastor finally confessed at a specially called meeting of the local church-governing body—the session—that his breakups were triggered by certain words in the Bible. *Shalt* was one, and *verily* was another. He had never had this problem before, he said, but "didn't *verily* sound kind of funny?"

The session let out a collective sigh and asked him to make a list of all the words that set him off. And when the Scripture lesson for that Sunday contained any of them, they asked the Worship Committee to get a volunteer to read the passages for him. They also insisted that he get some counseling.

The first to volunteer for the Scripture-reading job was Camilla Tumley, a ditsy housewife who appeared to have eaten too many salads. And while she was a sincere and dedicated church member, all of her spigots weren't quite open. She was— to put it kindly—confused.

Camilla taught Sunday school, and one morning astonished her high-school helper by telling the children that the images on Mount Rushmore had been made by God.

The dippy little lady had been a baton twirler in high school and had tried to carry over that kind of excitement into her adult life. She liked to say that after her weekly dose of listening to "The Flight of the Bumble Bee" she was quite out of breath.

So despite the fact that Camilla only had an attention span of a minute and a half, the Worship Committee agreed for her to take off from her teaching chores to read the Scripture lesson one Sunday morning. Most of the group figured that she was so delightfully dense that she wouldn't know what she was reading, and anyhow, she wouldn't appreciate the situation and would therefore be impervious to it.

But there is nothing more tempting than the possibility of laughter in a forbidden setting. Presbyterian worship services are deadly earnest events. There is decorum. Reverence and sobriety rule. There is little deviation from this atmosphere.

But humor is difficult to control. Any attempt to stifle merriment simply encourages it, for there is a contagion in laughter. One laugh begets others. It's like yawning: once it begins, it's dangerous.

By now the congregation was aware of the problem, of course, and of the words that caused it. Those who liked to follow along with the Scripture reading using the pew Bibles could see when one of the words was coming up. And many would snicker in anticipation.

Their noises reached out to Camilla, and while she looked puzzled, she began to giggle in response to their giggles. And when she reached one of the words, the congregation glanced over at the Minister (who had a knuckle in his mouth to try to stifle his own merriment), and that set them (and by extension, Camilla) off, filling the sanctuary with restrained chuckles.

Well, if naiveté couldn't overcome the problem, perhaps overkill would, so the Worship Committee then asked Earl Dorr to read the Scripture lesson the next time the words came up. Earl had been a shoe salesman for more than fifteen years. And, unlike his fellow members, he had an antic wit and a lot of jokes and old one-liners, which served him well in his profession and in his church life.

The wisecracker liked to tell the parishioners at the coffee hour that his luck was so bad that even yo-yos wouldn't come back to him! He said he often got sick on his day off! And he told anyone who would listen that when he was young, he was so poor that he could only have one measle at a time! You could almost hear the *bada boom* on the drums after each one of his comedy-club-like sallies.

As a shoe salesman, he maintained that he spent so much time on his knees that he ought to turn Catholic. That way, he said, he could maybe get to see the Virgin Mary's face in the bathroom of that auto-parts store in Progresso, Texas.

Earl was never at a loss for words. So he confidently agreed to the Worship Committee's request that he read the Scripture lesson on a Sunday morning. He had no problem with "the words." He didn't think they were funny at all, and he said he knew something about being funny!

But when the first giggle drifted up to him as he stood in the pulpit, he glanced up with a wary look. When another came at him, he became non plussed. This was not a little old lady trying on a size 7B and listening to his palaver. This was an audience!

Earl took the bait and began to exaggerate the text and smile and gesture and move about in the pulpit. As the congregation reacted with more giggles and chuckles, he fed on that and really began to ham it up. And when he got to one of "the words," he was on a roll and so overcome with glee and the wonderful reaction of his audience that he could do nothing but laugh out loud—and sit down.

The session met again—this time in a panic! The Minister reported no progress from the psychiatric sessions he was attending. No one had any more ideas. So finally the top dog of the session, the Clerk, decided that enough was enough. He, Elder Clarence T. Honchentruly, would take over.

Honchentruly was a cheerless accountant by profession and a dull, stern, and pious man who looked as if he had been in a bad mood all of his life. He had been a member for more than forty years and had served the congregation in many capacities, including two terms as head of the session. His philosophy was simple. He believed in the old saw that what is good is not new, and what is new is not good.

No one had ever seen him without his old-fashioned starched shirt collar and black string tie, and he held up his stockings with garters that wound around the long underwear he wore—even in the summer. He had an Old Testament look about him and a brook-no-nonsense countenance. No one ever called him by a name other than Mr. Honchentruly. And he harrumphed a lot.

At the time of the laughter problem, he was a ramrod-straight ancient who had retired none too soon. He was so old that Earl Dorr joked that Mr. Honchentruly was probably around when the Dead Sea Scrolls were only sick.

Peering balefully at the world over the top of his rimless glasses, he would draw himself up into a dignified posture at the sign of any levity. No one had ever seen him *listen* to a joke, let alone *tell* one.

And this thing about laughing during the Scripture lesson was out of control! It had to be curtailed!

So at an emergency meeting of the session, he pulled out his ever-present Bible and quoted 1 Corinthians 14:33: "For God is not the author of confusion." And in a passage dear to the hearts of his fellow Presbyterians, he read verse 40 from the same chapter, "Let all things be done decently and in order." There were a lot of "amens" to that, and all of those present nodded to each other in a vigorous manner.

Mr. Honchentruly said that he would put a stop to all this nonsense once and for all. He would break this humor habit by reading from the Scriptures himself the next time one of those words was in one of the passages to be read on a Sunday!

So he set out to fulfill his promise. As he rose and approached the pulpit on that Sabbath, there was tension in the sanctuary. The congregation had heard of Mr. Honchentruly's vow and was deadly silent and especially attentive. Here was their savior, come to do battle and smite the hilarity devil!

As he began the reading, there was a titter in the back, but he silenced that person with a scowl. And as he continued, he seemed to gather strength. His voice became stronger and more self-assured. He pressed on with confidence.

But as he approached one of the dangerous words, he began to falter. Three passages before it, he began to slow down and take deep breaths. A glimmer of a smile was seen to cross his face, and his voice became strangulated. Was he stifling a laugh?

From the right side of the sanctuary came a little giggle and then another from up front, near the choir. The Minister in his chair beside the pulpit was having a hard time keeping a straight face. Some chuckles floated up to Mr. Honchentruly as he got closer to the word, and it became apparent to the congregation that he was struggling to control himself.

Two passages before it, he gave way to a little snort himself, and that brought a further response from the congregation. A communal wave of glee was building.

He fought it and his own emotions. He cleared his throat. He looked to the ceiling. He gripped the sides of the pulpit tightly.

But when he finally reached the passage with the word in it, he paused, dropped his head, and emitted a resigned sigh. The absurdity of it all had finally reached him. As he read on, a sort of beatific grin spread over his face. He was giving up. The struggle was over. He could contain himself no longer.

From somewhere in his nether regions, a rumbling roar started, and when he got to the word *verily*, it erupted into a bellowing guffaw that engulfed him and rolled out over the congregation. They responded with a cacophony of laughter that threatened to bring down the walls!

Gone! They were all gone! Some folks bent over with tears streaming down their cheeks, while others clung to one another in abandonment. A few staggered to their feet, their faces contorted with hilarity, as they tried to make it to the exits.

At the pulpit, Mr. Honchentruly was helpless himself as he alternately bent over and pounded the railings with his fist, or leaned back in joyous roaring surrender to the demons that possessed him! Holding his sides, he finally fell to the floor, unable to stand upright in the face of the laughter that consumed them all! The Minister joined him there!

The congregation's howling continued for ten minutes, and after a few moments of giggling silence, started up again for another five minutes. The Choir Director finally took charge and canceled the rest of the service.

Some church historians in later years said that this local phenomenon of hysterics was but a precursor of the "holy laughter" manifestation, which arose in the 1990s. Often called The Toronto Blessing, this controversial worship service includes uncontrolled laughter, weeping, jerking, falling down, and speaking in tongues. It has become popular in some Pentecostal and Charismatic churches, but it has never been—nor probably ever will be—the type of a service held in a Presbyterian church.

Certainly not in that church in Ohio. The Minister Who Laughed left the week after the incident and eventually found an administrative job at a synod where he didn't have to read publicly from the Bible. A series of visiting preachers finally broke the humor chain.

And after an interim pastor, the Pastoral Nominating Committee (PNC) at the Ohio church recommended (and the church finally hired) an elderly minister who claimed that he hadn't had a humorous thought since 1964. So although he sometimes couldn't remember to shave both sides of his face, he got along fine with everybody and never even cracked a smile until his retirement five years later.

Word about the incident spread among Presbyterian churches throughout the land, and PNCs took it as a valuable lesson. Nowadays many of them try to remember to quiz every candidate for a ministerial position THOROUGHLY. They seek to make sure the person has never been to a comedy club, seen a sitcom, or read a funny book. It seems to save everybody a whole lot of trouble.

And of course, it is in keeping with the negative interpretation of the recently discovered Eleventh Commandment, in the Dead Sea Scrolls. "Thou Shalt NOT Laugh." It follows the gloomy translation by one of the professors.

But what if—just what if—that translation is wrong? What if the ancient writing is an admonition to laugh? What if the other professor is right? What if it says, "Thou SHALT Laugh"?

The scholar who favors the positive version of the command-ment maintains that God has a sense of humor. He quotes from Psalm 2: "He that sitteth in the heavens shall laugh." And he cites the fact that, according to the Bible, we are all made in God's image. If we laugh, He must laugh. And as far as we know, we are the only one of His creatures that CAN laugh.

Perhaps "the wisdom of this world is foolishness with God." After all, St. Francis of Assisi gave his followers the name "Jesters of Joy." Maybe—just maybe—the newly discovered Eleventh Commandment is an instruction to engage in merri-ment! What if we HAVE been directed to laugh?

Maybe there SHOULD be some buoyant laughter among our too-often pious posturings. Maybe we SHOULD enrich our souls by envisioning a little pimple of healthy humor on the nose of our beliefs. Maybe Reinhold Niebuhr had it right: "Humor is the prelude to faith, and laughter the beginning of prayer."

And perhaps, as Mark Twain once noted, when we remember that we are all mad, the mysteries disappear and life stands explained.

Scripture References
Used in Stories

Story 2: The Snowflake and the Church Bell

"Be glad then, ye children of Zion, and rejoice in the LORD your God: for he hath given you the former rain moderately, and he will cause to come down for you the rain, the former rain, and the latter rain in the first month" (Joel 2:23).

Story 4: Too Fat for Paopao

"Let every soul be subject unto the higher powers" (Romans 13:1).

"We ought to obey God rather than men" (Acts 5:29).

"Submit yourselves to every ordinance of man for the Lord's sake" (1 Peter 2:13).

"Owe no man any thing, but to love one another: for he that loveth another hath fulfilled the law" (Romans 13:8).

"Who shall go over the sea for us, and bring it unto us, that we may hear it, and do it?" (Deuteronomy 30:13).

"The doers of the law shall be justified" (Romans 2:13).

"But that no man is justified by the law in the sight of God" (Galatians 3:11).

"And lead us not into temptation" (Matthew 6:13).

"My brethren, count it all joy when ye fall into divers temptation" (James 1:2).

"Happy is the man that findeth wisdom, and the man that getteth understanding" (Proverb 3:13).

"Wisdom is the principal thing; therefore get wisdom; and with all thy getting get understanding" (Proverbs 4:7).

"For in much wisdom is much grief: and he that increaseth knowledge increaseth sorrow" (Ecclesiastes 1:18).

"For by grace are ye saved through faith: . . . it is the gift of God, not of works" (Ephesians 2:8–9).

"By works a man is justified, and not by faith only" (James 2:24).

"Take heed . . . do not sound a trumpet before thee" (Matthew 6:1–2).

"Let your light so shine before men, that they may see your good works, and glorify your Father which is in heaven" (Matthew 5:16).

"For I the LORD thy God am a jealous God, visiting the iniquity of the fathers upon the children" (Exodus 20:5).

"The son shall not bear the iniquity of the father" (Ezekiel 18:20).

"Answer a fool according to his folly, lest he be wise in his own conceit" (Proverbs 26:5).

"Answer not a fool according to his folly, lest thou also be like unto him" (Proverbs 26:4).

"Behold, how good and how pleasant it is for brethren to dwell together in unity" (Psalm 133:1).

Story 6: Meanwhile, Back at the Manse

"John the Baptist did eat locusts and wild honey" (Mark 1:6).

Story 7: The Eleventh Commandment

"The wisdom of this world is foolishness with God" (1 Corinthians 3:19).

About the
Author

Bob Reed is a proud native of Marcus, Iowa (pop. 1,171), who spent twenty-five years building and managing public television stations and as an executive at PBS. He has also served as a publisher and professor and has penned a lot of dull, scholarly research tomes, including an encyclopedia and a dictionary.

He is a navy veteran and proud grandfather who plays that happiest of instruments, the banjo. But as his wife, Max, often reminds him, the difference between a banjo player and a treasury bond is that eventually the bond matures and makes money.

Bob was raised a Methodist, was married in the Congregational Church, and is now a member of the Winter Park First Presbyterian Church in Florida. But even though he sings in the choir, they won't let him play the banjo at Sunday morning services.

In addition to his nonfiction works, he has published another book in this vein, *The Potluck Dinner That Went Astray—and Other Tales of Christian Life* (Smyth and Helwys), as well as a merry manual celebrating the funny foibles of his own denomination, *How to Survive Being a Presbyterian!* (iUniverse).

He thinks his very presence on this earth is proof that God has an unusual sense of humor. And he's certain that heaven is Iowa!

Bob Reed can be reached at reedgordon@aol.com

Printed in the United States
By Bookmasters